PRESENTING FINANCING PROPOSALS TO BANKS

Second Edition

Christopher A Bloomfield

Butterworths
London, Dublin & Edinburgh
1991

United Kingdom	Butterworth & Co (Publishers) Ltd, 88 Kingsway, LONDON WC2B 6AB and 4 Hill Street, EDINBURGH EH2 3JZ
Australia	Butterworths Pty Ltd, SYDNEY, MELBOURNE, BRISBANE, ADELAIDE, PERTH, CANBERRA and HOBART
Canada	Butterworths Canada Ltd, TORONTO and VANCOUVER
Ireland	Butterworth (Ireland) Ltd, DUBLIN
Malaysia	Malayan Law Journal Sdn Bhd, KUALA LUMPUR
New Zealand	Butterworths of New Zealand Ltd, WELLINGTON and AUCKLAND
Puerto Rico	Equity de Puerto Rico, Inc, HATO REY
Singapore	Malayan Law Journal Pte Ltd, SINGAPORE
USA	Butterworth Legal Publishers, AUSTIN, Texas; BOSTON, Massachusetts; CLEARWATER, Florida (D & S Publishers); ORFORD, New Hampshire (Equity Publishing); ST PAUL, Minnesota; and SEATTLE, Washington

A CIP Catalogue record for this book is available from the British Library.

First edition 1986

ISBN 0 406 00282 7

Printed by Dotesios Limited

PREFACE

I welcome the opportunity of this second edition, not just to review the text of the first edition but also to add certain sections covering topics which I was unable to include initially but now am able so to do.

Since writing the first edition, I am now what some people may well describe as gamekeeper turned poacher (or possibly bandit). I have left the halls of merchant banking as a director and now visit them only as a guest or a potential customer of the institution, normally with a client. I spend most of my time assisting entrepreneurs to raise finance for projects. This reversal of roles has involved me in many different projects with extremely wide and varied objectives but this has only served to reinforce my belief that the first step in a successful financing is a good presentation.

Such a reorientation has also led me to consider that there are other aspects of proposals which would benefit from being discussed at the time of constructing a proposition, even though they may not be implicitly stated in the documentation, and I have sought to cover this in the two new chapters which I have included in this edition.

There is no doubt that marketplaces are dynamic and the marketplace where finance is bought and sold is no exception to this, as we can easily see when looking back at the changes since 1986. Supply and demand have not always been in equilibrium and I am sure that these anomalies will continue in the future, making it either relatively easier or more difficult to get a particular project funded, depending upon the timing of the presentation. Obtaining finance can be a competitive business but this merely serves to emphasise that to give a project the best chance of success a little planning at the documentation stage can ensure a fair hearing.

Christopher Bloomfield
May 1991

CONTENTS

INTRODUCTION

There normally comes a time in the lives of most businesses when they have to ask a financial institution for money particularly in today's difficult trading climate. This can be the result of many different circumstances and sometimes it is only a short-term requirement bridging the receipt of funds from some project or delayed sale. However, it is often a request for finance to undertake some fundamental change in the business and requires the period of funding to be of a more permanent nature over several or even tens of years. These requests can appear to be a daunting procedure for any businessman but they fall into perspective if it is appreciated what a financial institution is looking for in any particular application and what sorts of criteria are applied to different types of financing instruments.

As with other types of requests the most effective are those which succeed first time; indeed it could be argued that generally there is only one opportunity to ask, that is first of all before any stances have been taken and before any prejudices have become set. It is as well to remember that financial institutions are run by human beings and generally these are called bankers although not always. I use the more general term 'financial institutions' rather than 'banks' to illustrate the point that money comes from many sources not just banks. Therefore throughout this book whenever the two terms are used it can be assumed that they are interchangeable unless it is specified otherwise. It might seem difficult to reconcile but these bankers do have their own peculiarities and foibles with likes and dislikes just as the rest of us do and these can impair their ability to see things clearly. First impressions do count and it is therefore important that any proposal has certain attributes, namely:

- CLARITY OF THOUGHT

- DEFINITE OBJECTIVES
- REASONED ARGUMENT
- EASE OF APPRECIATION

These obviously have to be incorporated into a formal structure and this is frequently referred to as a business plan but there are two separate elements here, the request for finance and the business plan. The latter is supporting evidence for the former and should be used as such. It is usual to incorporate the request for finance into the front of a business plan but it should be clearly identified.

As mentioned before there are numerous reasons why a business needs finance and there are already several aids to preparing business plans; however these in practice often amount to no more than a list of items to be included. What they do not give is a feel for the relative importance and weighting that should be attached to each of these items when seeking a particular form of finance. Clearly it is of little importance concentrating on the yield of a preference share when you are seeking to obtain mortgage finance for some factory development. Nevertheless it might not be quite so obvious why a bank would wish to understand fully to which suppliers money is owed when the request is for some form of invoice discounting facility. However, the bank will be concerned because if there are common suppliers and customers then there is the risk of setting off of accounts which can independently reduce the value of the debts held by the bank against which it has advanced funds.

It is exactly the same as filling in a tax return — if you only follow instructions as to which entries to make in each box then the chances are that you run the risk of not obtaining the most favourable assessment. It is much more effective to understand how you are to be assessed and thereby arrange your affairs to ensure that it produces the maximum benefit to you.

The purpose of this book is to assist the person who probably for the first time finds it necessary to make a formal proposal to a financial institution. It gives an insight into how institutions take decisions and how this can be used to best advantage when constructing a business plan. It provides the applicant with the maximum opportunity to ensure that his application receives full consideration on the terms which he wishes.

It is not uncommon for an application to take two to three weeks of fairly hard work as well as a lot of research to complete. For it to fall down because it is poorly presented is not only a misuse of resources, it is nothing more than gross negligence. For a small investment in time and a little diligent consideration that situation can be avoided. Success can never be guaranteed in any venture, including asking for money, because certain factors are always outside the sphere of control of the applicants, but if failure occurs for reasons other than these there must be a general question mark over the suitability of the applicant to manage his business prudently anyway.

A further consideration is that if you understand how an institution will view the risks involved you can get an appreciation of the type of financing that you should be seeking and ensure that you can identify and approach an institution which can provide such a package. Not all institutions provide the same facilities and even if they do not all of them can provide them equally effectively from the client's viewpoint. It is therefore essential that you can identify what you want and to whom you should go to obtain it.

The final part of the equation is that having decided what you want and who can give it to you it is well to appreciate what they are going to want in return. This too can vary considerably not only from transaction to transaction but also from institution to institution. Everyone wants something but they often have different reasons for seeking it. For one institution a running yield might be an essential condition for any provision of funds. For another it is regarded as a useful feature but could easily be negotiable if circumstances required.

I have already suggested that at first sight this can all appear very daunting but it should always be remembered that financial institutions are professional risk-takers. They can only make money by taking risks. That is the reward for their expertise in being able to discern what are the risks they wish to underwrite and then providing the funds to allow the investment to take place. Whether it is a high street clearing bank or a specialised investment fund, if money is not invested or lent by these institutions they are failing their shareholders in what they have set out to do. They exist to invest money prudently in acceptable ventures and therefore if you have chosen correctly you start off with a distinct advantage. Even though they might withdraw from the marketplace from time to time in the long term they want to try to provide you with funds if they possibly can. If you have a sound proposal and they are unable to support it that situation is as much their loss as it is yours.

Chapter 1

THE BANK'S DECISION-MAKING PROCESS

How a bank approaches a proposal

The current short-term uncertainty and difficulty being experienced in the financial sector disguises the longer-term trend which is that banking has now become an aggressive business and banks are generally hungry to lend money to sound projects. There has been intense competition in the high street for a share of the conventional lending market and this competition has grown up mainly as a result of the influence of overseas banks moving into the London market since the early 1970s. There are now over 400 foreign banks in London compared with less than 50 in the early 1970s. These, having come in to trade primarily in the wholesale market such as the inter-bank market, then began to look around at the retail sector as an attractive way of increasing earnings. Similarly, over about the same period there has been a rapid rise in the number of funds and institutions willing to undertake development capital investments. There are now over 200 of these institutions compared with only a handful operating during the mid 1970s. The result is that logically there should be no problem obtaining funds for a sensible proposition. However the recent poor trading experience of banks has led to them adopting a more cautious stance with credit assessment making it all the more important to present a proposal to its best possible advantage. Communication between the banker and the client must allow information to be imparted in a form which is understood by them both so that the risks and rewards of the proposal are clearly identified and can be evaluated easily. Whenever there is a loss of clarity in a proposal there is the risk of misinterpretation and uncertainty. The banker's task is to assess propositions and decide whether they conform to his institution's appetite for risk and reward. It therefore follows that the more uncertainty that enters into any proposition then the higher the risk factor. This leads to two possible reactions to the proposal. Either the perceived higher risk causes the proposition to move into a different risk category, which for the institution concerned is one where it will not underwrite business, or alternatively, if it is still in a risk category where the institution will operate, then to balance the required risk reward ratio it is necessary to increase the reward element to match the higher assessment of risk.

I hope this short analysis makes it perfectly clear why the need for correct communication with a bank is critical when seeking funding.

The stages in an application for finance

The preparation of an application and presentation of it to a financial institution are important parts of the stages in obtaining finance but they are by no means the only ones. They are the first steps but there are many more stages which occur and an appreciation of these later events can be of assistance in the approach taken at the beginning when constructing the application.

They are as follows:

- the company perceives a financial requirement
- the company prepares a presentation for the bank
- the bank provides an initial response and requests further information
- the bank's case officer prepares a proposition for submission to the bank's sanctioning authority
- sanction is obtained
- investigation work is concluded
- documentation
- completion pre-conditions met and money goes out
- review and development of relationship

The company perceives a financial requirement

This is an essential step in any presentation but simple as it may seem there have been many occasions when I have received a company's presentation which was unclear as to what its financial requirement was. This resulted in a stream of undirected facts being presented to the banker and he was then left to decide what it was that he was being asked to do. This should not be his job — he does not run the company, you do. Therefore if you are unclear as to what you need, unless it is a legitimate case of exploring what might be possible, which it very rarely is, then the chances are you will not get what you want and the whole of the ensuing arguments will be wasted. The essence of making a presentation to a bank is that it is driven by the company. The bank should be in a reactive situation, ideally only having to evaluate the soundness of the arguments being proposed. When a bank's position moves from reactive to proactive then you have lost the initiative and there is a possibility that the deal you have been seeking will not be forthcoming. It is exactly the same as any other selling operation; the prospect must be carried at every step of the presentation. If it founders early on then that throws into doubt the validity of all the subsequent points no matter how well they may be founded because they will be considered to have been based upon erroneous assumptions.

It is therefore critical that the financial requirement is clearly defined and identified both in terms of how much it amounts to when reviewed in monetary terms and how it comes to have arisen. The second part of this is helpful in allowing the bank to appreciate the nature of the requirement, which will vary in its permanency depending on the situation that the company finds itself in. In other words, how quickly the company can generate such sufficient cash flow to repay/redeem facilities without jeopardising the business. There should be no doubt in the bank's mind what it is that it is being asked for, why the company has need of it, how long they will wish to make a facility available and what the nature of that facility will be. If these questions can be answered clearly that will provide a sound base to move on to the next part of the process.

The company prepares a presentation for the bank

Having decided that you need some money the next stage is to argue why it should be given to you. This is best done with a written presentation and there are several good reasons for this. Firstly, a banker, like most other people, does not like being presented with facts at the same time as he is expected to react to them and ask questions about them. It is more acceptable and more professional to provide the figures ahead of the meeting so that due consideration can be given to the arguments and the assumptions and that questions can be carefully directed and not fired off without having a grasp of the full picture. It is also a much more efficient way of conducting a meeting and a more effective way of presenting a case. A positive response will normally only come if a banker is confident about his understanding of the business and his grasp of the requirements. If there are areas of uncertainty these are best explored with a complete knowledge of the facts as presented. This is because often the uncertainty is more understandable when presented as part of a whole picture and can be quantified as to its likely impact upon the business. Whereas if only a partial understanding is present, it is human nature to assume the worst and any particularly soft areas expand to include in their downside the worst about the areas in which there is no understanding at all but which may be covered later in the proposal. Secondly, banks are well aware of the emotional element that can be present in listening to someone making a presentation. It is very easy to get swept along with the enthusiasm of the moment and make some rash decision which is later regretted in the cold light of day. I certainly have lived to regret occasions like that, and I know that I am not alone, and therefore there is a tendency to guard against this by stalling and refusing to be drawn when asked leading questions. The maxim that is often followed and which makes good sense is not to make a decision at any meeting but to go back to your office and think about it. This means that a meeting will not be as constructive as it could be unless a banker is at his ease with the discussion and the way in which it is going. This is best achieved by familiarity and this can only be obtained by presenting a proposal in good time and in such a manner that it can be clearly understood.

There will be considerable discussion later on as to how a proposal should be prepared, what it should contain and how it should be structured. What it is important to appreciate initially is why it should be prepared at all and why a verbal presentation will probably not fulfil the objectives of the business in an effective manner.

The bank provides an initial response and requests further information

The initial response is the first hurdle in the progress of a successful application through a bank and is determined by the result of several factors, some of which are highly subjective. The aim of the applicant should be to reduce the subjective element to a minimum and ensure that coherent argument becomes the overriding element in determining the banker's reaction. Financing proposals come into banks through different routes. Some are sent directly to known individuals, others come via professional firms such as accountants or solicitors; but through whichever door they actually arrive, inevitably they gravitate towards the bank's representative in the appropriate department, whose task it is to consider new proposals. Sometimes this section is called a new business department or a marketing department and the title of the bank official can vary — manager, director, account officer, or executive. It does not really matter what his or her title is; if the job is to look at new business then he will almost certainly be working to a very tight schedule and will have to be in a position to make decisions at a very early stage following a proposal's appearance within his organisation. The particular power of this position is often not that of acceptance but one of rejection. It normally means that he can determine whether a proposal shall be proceeded with or not. This particular skill is one which the bank values very highly. If he were not there then the organisation would begin to slow down and eventually stop, being choked up with proposals that were being pursued but which there was no possibility of the bank ever wishing to complete. Some idea of the importance of this function can be obtained when considering the level of conversion into completed transactions that institutions expect to achieve from proposals. An institution that was looking at equity investments only might expect to convert no more than 5 per cent of all introductions into transactions on its books. With a pure lending institution the conversion rate would increase somewhat, but not to the level where it would be worthwhile for the bank to pursue every transaction past its initial introduction.

It is worthwhile, therefore, to take a little time to ensure that the needs of this particular individual are met, and in the light of being able to understand what his job entails it becomes easier to structure a document providing him with the information he requires in a form he can easily assimilate. If this is not done then you will be increasing the odds against you purely for lack of preparation, an area entirely within your own control.

It should be realised that with the levels of conversion rates that I have indicated he will not have unlimited time available to consider every application in detail. A decision will have to be made on the basis of the overall picture that is presented, taking into consideration in particular what the major risk areas are and what the potential for reward is. If there are any areas which are uncertain the bank's representative will draw upon his existing knowledge of that area which may be either relevant or not, depending on the individual. This can very easily work to the disadvantage of an applicant and therefore any proposal should be read before submission with these points in mind. It is possible that he may have some form of technical expertise outside that of finance, but it is unlikely, and even if he does he will only have a general knowledge because he will not have been working in that field for some time. It is much better to assume that he is going to read the proposal from the standpoint of an intelligent layman. When it comes to understanding your business no one will know it as well as you do and therefore you should make allowances for this when describing it.

If the proposal is initially attractive to the bank's officer he will normally request a meeting to discuss it. Otherwise he will write or telephone to say that it is not one which he feels they wish to pursue. This first meeting can serve several purposes. It gives the bank a feel for the people they are being asked to help, albeit a very superficial one. It nevertheless allows the bank to hear the document explained by the people who are going to make it work. And here it is probably as well to give a word of warning. It is quite possible to get an application entirely prepared by various professional firms and this can produce a very good document. If care is not exercised it is possible that this produces something that is 'too slick'. This itself can be very offputting for a banker. Professional input is useful, sometimes essential, in a presentation but it must be the management's plan. It becomes very clear to a banker when talking with management just what their input has been in the preparation of the plan and how committed they are to it. In the final analysis it does not matter how many external advisers say that the plan will work. If the management do not believe it and are not committed to it then it will be unlikely that a banker will finance it. Therefore make sure that it is your plan which you are explaining to the bank and not somebody else's version of what you should be doing.

At the initial meeting with the bank, and hopefully there should be several more, it is probably best if only the chief executive and financial director attend. This ensures that there is an adequate level of support without making the meeting of unmanageable size. There will be plenty of time later for the bank to meet the other key members of the executive team if it is appropriate.

A further reason for this first meeting from the bank's point of view is that, if the document has been received at an early enough stage, it allows the bank to probe and question any areas where it feels uncertain. This will inevitably occur. It is impossible to include sufficient information in a proposal to ensure that every aspect has been covered to everyone's satisfaction. Indeed, if this were the case it could only be achieved by assuming a knowledge level of zero and producing a document that was so comprehensive it was completely unwieldy and lacked the focus and direction which is essential in an application for finance. This questioning is important because generally people who do not have questions to ask are not really interested in what they are hearing. This is true of banks as it is of individuals. Questions need not be regarded with suspicion. Bankers generally are simple people who, individual personality aberrations apart, are interested in doing deals and not in asking clever questions to score points. If a question is asked then it should be taken at face value and responded to as such, preferably in a confident manner. The banker generally does not know the answer to the questions he is asking. If he regards it as important and if you answer it in a way that implies unreasonable doubt in your own mind then he will not feel particularly confident in basing his own arguments for underwriting this transaction upon your response. Obviously there are occasions when a question is asked to which a quantitative reply cannot be given but care should be taken to explain why this is so and also why it need not be a problem when considering your proposal. What does not inspire confidence is the sort of glib reply which most of us who discuss proposals with clients have at some times suffered. It goes along the following lines:

'Well, how many of these items do you think you should be able to sell over the next year?' Response: 'As many as we can make, old boy!'

This is not particularly helpful because it leaves so many questions unanswered. By implication the market size is greater than production capacity but no explanation is given as to why this should be so nor even what maximum production capacity is.

Ideally the information gleaned during the first meeting should enable the banker to make his initial evaluation of the proposal and possibly to give you an idea of the sort of indicative terms, without commitment, that he considers the institution should be capable of making available if everything else works out. This can be extremely useful both from the bank's viewpoint and from the client's. It enables them both to assess whether they wish to pursue the issue any further. One meeting is rarely sufficient for a bank to decide to undertake a transaction unless it is extremely simple but from the bank's viewpoint it is a considerable investment in time which represents a substantial amount of money and there is little point moving on to the next stage unless the client is going to be happy with the eventual likely outcome. From the client's side of the fence he is being given an opportunity to assess the bank's requirements and I would make the point that the terms given at this stage would very rarely improve as time goes on. The reason for this is that the assumptions that have been made are based on the understanding that everything in the business plan is capable of being substantiated and that the current state of knowledge is perfect. This is not the case and subsequent investigation can reveal further weaknesses which cause the original terms to be amended to take account of these discrepancies. However, this is a basis on which to assess terms and conditions, particularly if more than one institution is being approached.

On the assumption that the bank's terms are broadly acceptable, it is then normal for the bank's representative to come out and visit the company on its own premises. This is a useful process for the banker in that it puts flesh on the bones of the proposal in a way that words on a page can never do. If the meeting is arranged in a constructive manner it enables him to gain a first-hand impression of the company's operations, how its business looks, the physical attributes of any processes and the personalities involved in the day-to-day running. There is no substitute for going to see a client on his own ground. It is probably worth observing that if a banker does not know you and is not prepared to come and visit your business then you should not be considering taking your proposal with that institution any further. If there is such little interest being shown when there is time to learn, should things ever get difficult it would be unwise to rely upon that institution for a sympathetic understanding of the problems besetting the business.

From the banker's outlook there are other good reasons for going to see a client, not least because most institutions have stories about facilities being made available to finance such assets as properties etc. without the site ever having been visited. Eventually the loan goes wrong and the bank goes down the road to view the building only to find that it has never been started, even though funds have been advanced. There are plenty of variations on this theme but they all have one moral for the banker — get out and see what you are putting your money into. There is a further consideration which the client can use to his advantage in getting a banker to see his business for a day. It generally takes the best part of a day to undertake an effective visit to a client and get a better working knowledge of his business. This is quite a long time to be in the company of one person and you can begin to get an idea of whether or not you are likely to be able to get on and work together. This is a most important consideration and one which should never be forgotten. Once a facility has been made available the client will normally be liaising with the bank through this particular representative. If there are significant problems with personalities or approaches these are going to make an efficient working relationship harder to obtain.

The bank's case officer prepares a proposition for submission to the bank's sanctioning authority

Having undertaken his initial investigation the bank's representative will have satisfied himself that the request for finance is legitimate, ie it is borne out by the circumstances that the business finds itself in and the opportunities that have been presented to it. He will also be careful that the introduction of funds by the bank will enable the business to progress and achieve its objectives while not exposing the bank to unacceptable risk. His understanding of the operation will allow him to feel that the management team are capable of using this money in a way which will make the business projections occur and that they are capable of exercising the degree of stewardship and have the necessary integrity to enable him to feel confident in providing them with funds. It is then necessary for him to convey these confidences to his sanctioning authority.

As has been indicated previously, the bank's representative who deals with the new business applications does not necessarily have the authority to sanction a transaction. This is not at all unusual, as the level of sanctioning authority can vary from institution to institution and it will also probably vary from financial product to financial product so that an official who has a £500,000 level of authority for secured loans may well only have a £200,000 level of authority for a higher level of risk such as unsecured loans, and only have a £100,000 authority for equity-related risks such as buying shares in a business, which would be regarded as an even higher level of risk from the bank's point of view.

As a general rule, the more funds that are being requested then the more likely it is that the proposal will have to go on to another committee. It is quite possible in certain cases that it will have to go through two or three stages before it is actually sanctioned. While this is not unusual it can be disadvantageous to the client because each time it gets further away from the person who has first-hand knowledge of the business. It can be useful to ask the bank at the outset what its sanctioning process is and how it will have to react to your proposition if it is to be successful. From the answer you receive you will be able to decide whether it might be less effort to try another institution with shorter reporting lines.

It should now be clear that if you cannot convince your contact with the bank of the validity of your case he will be in a very poor position to convince his credit committee as to why they should carry out the transaction he is proposing. It is your job to ensure that he has the information available to convince his sanctioning authority. You must not rely upon him to do everything. It leaves you too vulnerable to interpretation. This is an area that can be controlled and should be tackled with this in mind. It is essential that the bank's representative is fully briefed and has access to all supporting information before he submits his proposal to the sanctioning authority.

Sanction is obtained

When sanction is obtained from an institution it very rarely is given in an absolute form unless the transaction is an extremely simple one. It is normally subject to several pre-conditions being met and to satisfactory completion of documentation.

The institution normally communicates sanction by writing a letter. Sometimes if there is already a facility in place the letter itself constitutes the documentation and merely varies the terms of the existing facility. Then all that has to be done is for the client to sign a copy of this letter and return it to signify his acceptance of terms and the facility is then made available at the agreed higher level. Otherwise the process will be a little more complicated. This letter will be the first stage in the documentation of the facility.

It is often called an offer letter and takes the form shown below. The precise terms included in this letter will be discussed later but at this stage it is the general format and outline that is being indicated.

> The Directors,
> Streetwise Trading Limited,
> Oxford
>
> Gentlemen;
>
> £5M TERM LOAN — TEN YEARS
>
> The Bank is pleased to confirm that it is prepared to make available a £5m term loan to Streetwise Trading Limited subject to completion of

documentation satisfactory to the bank, the principal terms of which are outlined below:

Borrower:	Streetwise Trading Limited
Amount:	£5,000,000
Period:	Ten years
Interest rate:	2 per cent plus Mandatory Liquid Asset Costs plus London Inter-Bank Offered Rate
Interest period:	Three months and six months
Repayment:	Five equal annual instalments of £1,000,000 to commence on the first anniversary of drawdown
Security:	Mortgage over the property over 3 Landshill Road, Oxford
Covenants:	Annual interest charge of Streetwise Trading Limited to be three times covered by profits before tax as shown in the audited accounts
	Total bank borrowings of Streetwise Trading Limited not to exceed 70 per cent of shareholders funds
Pre-condition:	Mortgage valuation of the property by a firm of valuers acceptable to the bank to show a valuation of not less than £7,000,000
Drawdown:	In one amount not more than 60 days after the date of this letter
Costs:	All costs including legal fees incurred by the bank to be paid by Streetwise Trading Limited whether or not the facility is drawn, these fees not to exceed £10,000 in total
Fees:	Arrangement fee of £5,000 to be payable to the bank on drawdown
Early repayment fee:	In the event of prepayment of the loan during the first five years. In this event there will be a charge of 1/2 per cent of the amount prepaid which will be payable by the company to the bank.

Can you please sign a copy of this letter and return it to the bank indicating your acceptance of these terms and conditions.

The reason for this type of letter is to ensure that there is no misunderstanding concerning the principal points of the facility before professional costs start to be incurred. It can be that a company is seeking two or three offer letters and wishes to assess them. This then is the point at which a decision has to be made concerning which institution it wishes to pursue. As will be noted from the terms of the letter, it is common for an institution to make it a condition that any fees incurred will be passed on to the customer and the customer agrees to meet these. This is an indication of a sign of interest by the customer in taking up the facility.

As a practical consideration, if you are happy with the terms sign a copy of the letter and return it but do not agree to pay any costs which cannot be quantified. If professional fees are going to be incurred by the bank insist that estimates of these are given by the professionals concerned before agreeing to meet them, or at least agree an upper limit above which any fees incurred by the bank will not be your responsibility.

Investigation work concluded

This stage is essentially the bank seeking verification, often by independent bodies, that the principal elements of the transaction are the same as those assumed in its argument for undertaking the transaction. This can take several forms but the most common are as follows:

Valuation of assets This is particularly important when considering security. If it has been agreed to lend against an anticipated realisable value of an asset, say 60 per cent of the sale value of a building, then it is usual, if there is not a recent valuation in existence, for the bank to ask for one from a firm of valuers in whom the bank has confidence. It does not just apply to buildings — it could be the value of the company's stock or an investigation into its method of valuing work in progress, particularly when a bank is trying to attribute value to a floating charge.

Accountant's investigation An accountant's investigation can be a very detailed review of the company's accounting policies, assets, liabilities, contracts and systems. This really depends on the letter of instruction which is given. This is normally drafted by the bank for the company to sign and then sent to an agreed firm of accountants. Its purpose is to verify areas that are critical to the facility being proposed and often will only cover one or two particular aspects such as the management information systems that are operating in the company or perhaps the costing systems that are being used.

Other less common requests but nevertheless appropriate to certain types of facilities are:

Market analysis of a company's products This can be necessary when a company is seeking money to develop a new product or expand into new areas of the same market. It can also be necessary when a company is too close to its own marketplace to take a broad view and anticipate the likely threats to its particular product range, or the way in which the marketplace it is selling into fits into the overall economic activity of the country or the world.

Product investigation If a request for financing involves a new method of production then it may well be appropriate for the bank to seek confirmation that the risks involved in this new operation are acceptable and that the skills to control it are within the company.

References Finally, if the company is not already known to the bank and it is seeking equity financing, personal references of the senior management may well be requested and followed through. In that type of transaction the bank is backing the management team completely without any assets to fall back on as security. If the management team cannot demonstrate that they are a team worth backing then they will probably not obtain the funds which they require.

Documentation

When sitting down and thinking about this stage it is always difficult to see why it should take very much time at all and quite often it does not. For a straightforward facility using standard documentation, often in the nature of pre-printed forms, documentation can be completed extremely quickly and with the minimum amount of fuss. For more complex transactions such as a management buy-out, where there are several transactions going on at the same time and several facilities being provided and at least three separate parties taking part, it can take weeks to get agreement on documentation. For larger transactions such as these all parties are advised by their own solicitors and it is often necessary to have several drafting meetings to obtain agreed documentation. The principal documents are a facility letter if it is a loan facility, or a shareholders agreement if the bank is subscribing for shares in the company. There will be other documents involved but these are the ones where the major points and agreements will be.

The important point to remember about drafting meetings, particularly if you are seeking professional advice, which I believe is sensible in most cases, is to be aware of what it is you are trying to do. At the end of the day it is you who is the person doing the deal and it is your commercial judgment that should decide in the end. A professional adviser can and should indicate what the potential risks in documentation are, but it is your decision as to whether you are prepared to accept those risks. I have been involved in several meetings where the original deal has been obscured by discussions over fine legal points.

Completion, pre-conditions met and money out

This is the most pleasant meeting of all from both parties' points of view. It can often take place at the bank's offices or, if it concerns the sale and purchase of a company, at the offices of the vendors' solicitors. It involves the signing of all documentation which should by now be agreed and evidence of pre-conditions being met. This could take the form of production of the valuation certificate or evidence of the directors having taken out keyman insurance to protect the company if anything happens to them. It could be the bank saying that it is satisfied with the references that it has taken up on the management team. It depends upon what the offer letter said about the conditions of making the facility available. Upon completion of all these points the funds are made available and a new relationship starts between the company and the bank.

Review and development of relationship

This is an important aspect of the whole process and where there can be a lot of benefits to be obtained from an institution. Once a relationship has been established it is important that the bank is kept informed at all times as to what is going on within the company.

There will probably have been an information clause in the facility letter where the company has undertaken to provide financial information on a regular basis and this in itself is important. However, if things are not going according to plan it is better to explain this to the bank earlier rather than later. This then allows the management team time for reflection and discussion with the institution about what would be the best course of action to be taken. Secondly, in the circumstances it is important that the management team suggest a course of action which they wish to have supported. Relying on the bank to dig them out is not a very good idea.

Even if things do not go wildly differently from what was intended it can still be a good practice to keep the bank well informed. It has taken a lot of effort to obtain and build a relationship with the bank. This effort need not be duplicated for further requests for finance, because if your relationship has been built properly then the bank starts off by being on your side and should feel more confident in being able to assess your request, be it for higher levels of trading or for capital expenditure plans. The getting-to-know-you process should not have to be gone through again. Similarly, the bank too has spent a considerable amount of its resources in obtaining you as a customer. It too wants to capitalise on this effort if it possibly can and providing further financial facilities in appropriate circumstances is one of the ways it can do so.

Chapter 2

FINANCING REQUIREMENTS

Types of financial requirements

Having discussed how a bank will approach a request for a facility, we can now continue to consider the types of financial requirement that a company might have and where they fit in the bank's perception of the business. Types of financing requirements vary considerably depending upon the purpose that they are to be used for and their size in relation to the business requiring them.

1 Trading and strategic requirements

The difference between trading and strategic requirements is important and can serve as a useful rule of thumb to determine how deeply a bank will need to look behind a proposal at the company and the management teams who are going to make it work.

A trading requirement for a company should by definition have certain attributes. It will be determined by the company's business; therefore it will in some shape or form be related to the buying or selling of goods and services and consequently the time cycle that it takes from buying and paying for the goods to selling and receipt of funds. The underlying principle here is that each transaction should be self-liquidating over a fairly short period of time, ie if money is borrowed to purchase goods then it is presumably intended that those goods will be sold at a profit; therefore, funds are generated upon sales to repay the facility. In practice this might be disguised by the fact that the company has moved on to a higher level of trading and that there are several transactions in process at any one time, and as it is repaid it is immediately replaced by another one and therefore overall the facility stays at a higher level. This is not unacceptable to the bank given that it is satisfied with its overall exposure to the company and this level, as long as it can be demonstrated that the facility is turning over regularly with profitable business. The concern from the bank's viewpoint is that it is financing a profitable business. In this event, if sales turn down then the company has a lower requirement for the facility because it will be purchasing less, and as the older contracts mature these funds flow into the bank account and reduce the facility automatically. If the business being financed is unprofitable then part of the facility will have been used to finance losses and upon liquidation there are insufficient funds generated to repay the facility. This leaves the bank in the unenviable position of having to decide whether it will continue to support the loss-making company by advancing further funds until it becomes profitable or call it a day and make demands upon the company for the money and if necessary realise security to allow repayment. This is a fairly extreme outcome but nevertheless it illustrates the risk which a bank incurs when it thinks it is financing a trading facility and then finds that it has become involved in strategic re-structuring of the business. The essential elements to bear in mind are self-liquidation of the facility and profitable trading.

As already indicated it could be that a company requires a trading facility but that this facility remains at a high level due to an increasing level of trade. The approaches that the bank can take in these circumstances can be several and not necessarily mutually exclusive. If the company is persistently profitable then in the longer term, regardless of any short-term accounting discrepancies, profitability should equal free cash flow. By that I mean money that would be available to repay the loan. If this flow is being generated fairly quickly then the bank may be content to leave things as they are and see a relatively small decline in the facility each year, or even allow it to remain constant, while the rest of the business increases in profitability. It is more likely, though, that because of increase in sales and working capital requirements the company will take some time to repay the facility, in which case the bank may feel that it wants to re-structure the facility and place it on a term basis, say for five or ten years with a structured repayment every year. Alternatively it could well be that the company would wish to raise equity finance to support the higher level of trading and replace what would be referred to as 'hardcore' borrowings.

It can be seen that these alternatives are different to the short-term facility in that they are not linked to the short-term trading position but to the longer-term strategic requirements of the business. It is this type of facility that will cause banks to look in depth at a company's financial position and products, when the financing is material and for a strategic purpose, and it is these types of transactions that will most often require a detailed presentation to be prepared before they can be given adequate consideration.

2 Strategic financial requirements in the life cycle of a company

To gain an appreciation of what these strategic requirements might be it is probably best to illustrate how they occur throughout the life cycle of the business. Naturally there will always be exceptions to the rule but it will serve to give a good outline of the type of transaction that we are talking about.

Small company stage:	- pre-production finance - start-up finance - development capital - management buy-out
Medium-size company:	- Growth can be achieved through:- - development capital - acquisition finance
Large/multi-national company:	- re-structuring - leveraged buy-outs - refi nancing debt maturities - fixed and variable rate debt - raising equity or bonds on capital markets

Before we consider these briefly, it is worth noting that in many cases the size of the requirement relative to the company's present position is such that a large proportion of funding should be raised by way of equity capital. When a company is quoted this will be obtained from the public by a recognised market such as the Stock Exchange. When it is unquoted this will have to be obtained from banks and other institutions who are prepared to consider taking equity stakes.

At the small company stage, particularly at the point of start-up, almost any financing requirement is strategic because everything has to be proved and there is no record to judge against.

The willingness or otherwise of a bank to put money into a start-up after satisfaction with the project and management itself will be the financial commitment of the management team, and while there are several banks willing to back start-ups no one likes financing 100 per cent of these situations. The commitment may not need to be large absolutely but it should be large in relation to the resources of the individual. Start-ups are high risk operations. Statistics indicate this and most equity finance houses investing in start-ups tend to support the view that one in three will fail. Start-up finance does not have to be equity but the ability of a bank to provide conventional loan finance will almost certainly depend purely upon the strength of covenant offered by the management team, ie the company will not justify it but external support in the form of additional adequate security may well allow conventional finance.

I have mentioned management buy-outs in this category because in some respects they are a start-up, but they can be for very large companies indeed and a variation on this, the leveraged buy-out, can be for companies valued at £100m or more.

For a medium-sized company there are probably more opportunities to incorporate conventional finance into a development package or acquisition package because these are basically the two alternatives for expansion — 'grow it yourself' or 'buy it'. It should be realised that even consolidation, ie strengthening the balance sheet and systems without undertaking dramatic increase in turnover, is to enable a company to undertake the next step of its plans with a more stable structure. Therefore re-financing an overdraft as a term loan as mentioned before is a strategic step.

Large organisations are likely to have strategic requirements arising out of re-structuring of their existing portfolio financing from acquisition or development plans. During the last ten years we have seen a growth in treasury departments for large companies within the UK, and the management of debt facilities has become a full-time job often independent of, although reporting to, the finance director. There are many considerations that have to be watched as external circumstances change, such as whether it is better to have, say, a long-term debt profile maturing evenly over the next 20 years or whether it is better to finance this by some fixed rate long-term debt and short-term floating rate debt, what currency exposures are being incurred and what action needs to be taken to limit them. All these are strategic considerations not immediately linked with the day-to-day trading requirements of the business.

3 Spectrum of financial transactions

There are many different types of financial products that are offered by banks today and they are viewed as falling at different points in the spectrum of financial risk. This is independent of the risk which any particular covenant might have attaching. For example, the two products, say a term loan and a preference share, provided to the same company, would have different pricing requirements because they would be standing at different levels in the financial risk spectrum.

Below I have indicated in order of descending risk various financial transactions and then I have described the products that might be used in structuring these transactions.

(1) Unquoted equity transactions

(a) Research and development finance
(b) Pre-production finance
(c) Start-up finance
(d) Development capital
(e) Management buy-outs
(f) Management buy-ins
(g) Money out deals

(2) Investment in quoted companies

(3) Conventional bank finance

(a) Strategic financing
(b) Trading finance

I have not dealt in any detail with the spread of transactions for investment in quoted companies because it is unlikely that anyone proposing such a venture would be reading a book such as this. However, suffice it to say that the type of instrument used in any quoted transactions will be similar to any of the other areas mentioned except that it will be possible to buy and sell such an instrument independently of the wishes of the company.

Although it is impossible to define a group of financial transactions exactly because they very rarely consist solely of one type of transaction or another type of transaction, it is worthwhile detailing the various unquoted equity transactions mentioned above because they seem to have fallen into common usage and most institutions mean more or less the same thing when they use them. The only point I would make is that you may often see the term 'venture capital' used in several different contexts. The broad definition of venture capital, which is the one used in the USA, covers all of the transactions mentioned under (1) above. In the UK it seems to have become rather more specific in that it is quite often used only to describe high risk start-up situations. Either way it does not really matter because the confusion disappears when you begin to describe potential transactions.

Risk spectrum for equity transactions

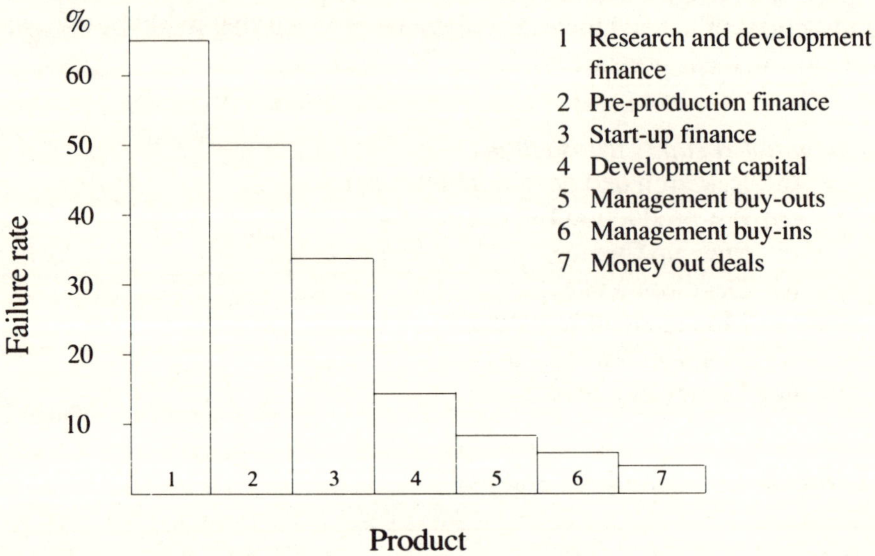

(a) Research and development finance

This is one of the highest areas of risk in terms of any financial transaction. It involves backing a team who have not yet identified a specific product or production process. These may be defined in terms of market area or type of process but they will not exist at this stage. It is unlikely that the management team exist who would bring the process to a commercial reality and there could be several rounds of further financing required before it reaches start-up stage.

Examples of this type of funding can be found in areas such as biotechnology. The investors could be looking at time scales as long as 10 to 15 years before any payback and certainly could expect no dividends for some considerable time. Normally only very specialised institutions would undertake this type of funding and it is often carried out in conjunction with a commercial organisation as a partner which has a strategic interest in developing the processes involved.

(b) Pre-production finance

Although one stage further on than the previous, this is still an area of high risk. Work may well have to be done on pre-production prototypes and there will be uncertainty attaching as to whether this product can actually be made. The management team may or may not exist. It depends really on the length of time that it is anticipated that these problems will take to resolve. Again further financing will probably be required before it can come to the marketplace. Both of these first two categories are in the position where, even if everything goes well, at the end of the day you do not have a product that is selling in the marketplace and which can be judged by its performance. It is still necessary to convince someone to put up further finance before any payback can be received from the existing investment.

(c) Start-up finance

Compared with the first two this is an easier situation to analyse. A management team should exist, the product should be in a form where it can be produced, it should already have been produced in a limited form and the full-scale production process should be clearly identified. Market analyses should have been undertaken and there should be a very clear idea about what it is the business will be doing and how it will obtain its objectives. Nevertheless, as we have mentioned previously, even at this stage one out of three start-ups are expected to fail, indicating that all the planning in the world is no substitute for being able to deliver the goods when it really counts.

At various stages in a company's life it is very fragile and no more so than when it is in the start-up situation. At the time when it needs them most it has limited resources and probably an over-stretched management team.

(d) Development capital

This particular heading indicates that funds are being provided to develop the business. This gives a clue as to the state that the company has already achieved. It is one of the most common of all requirements of financing and therefore warrants a little time being spent dealing with it. The company has passed the start-up stage and has reached a level where there is a record of its progress against which the performance of the management team can be judged and the financial standing of the business can be assessed. It has the added attraction of products that have been selling in existing markets and their success or otherwise can be quantified. Also they can be compared with products of competitors and opinions obtained from users as to their quality and proficiency. All in all it is a very different type of proposal from the first three we have mentioned. There is something to assess in the present, not just hopes for the future.

A development capital requirement arises when an existing business wishes to pursue a development in its business and the costs of the exercise are such that it cannot be funded by conventional means of finance, ie bank loans. It is important to realise that this exercise should be precisely what has just been described. It is not a total change in direction by a company or a frantic investment in a new product because the existing ones have only a year of life left in them. These might well appear to be development capital situations but they are not. It is probably easiest if it is remembered that a failure by the company to make a success of a development capital project should not result in the demise of the total business.

This presupposes an appropriate financing structure. For example, if the whole of the development project were funded by means of loan stock when the interest costs of the loan stock were equivalent to the existing profits of the business, then although the project that was being funded might be of a true development capital nature, the financing structure that has been chosen places the whole of the existing business at risk upon failure of the new project. This is a totally unacceptable position for a business to find itself in and if any such scheme is suggested by an institution then you should look elsewhere. The rationale must be that upon failure of the new project the enlarged business can be collapsed on to the old existing business and although this might be costly in shutdown costs such as redundancies, removals etc. it does not result in the collapse of the company. If the example above had been funded by one-third loan stock and two thirds equity then upon failure of the new development, assuming the business could still make approximately the same profits from its existing business, interest would be about three times covered by profits and this would represent a more balanced financial position than that where the business was just working to pay interest. It is important in any equity situation that the institution providing the fundings takes its share of the equity risk if it is taking a share of the equity reward. It might be tempting from a proprietor's point of view to say that you do not need equity funding, you can do it all on loans or something similar, but I would ask you to remember that history shows that there are as many stupid lenders as borrowers and you should not necessarily rely upon a bank to protect you from yourself in these circumstances. You must assess your own business, make your own appreciation of the risks involved and then decide whether the downside risks require a degree of equity investment.

I hope that by now it is becoming clear that although things are being labelled by convenient headings, nothing is ever that straightforward and with development capital you can very easily have a company that fits into the development capital mould — it is established and has a good record — but is not seeking to undertake a development capital risk. An example has already been cited where for financial structuring reasons alone the risks moved into a higher level than should be necessary for a development capital transaction. Similarly, considerations of size can have the same sort of effect. A business may well have a good record but if it wishes to undertake an investment project that involves raising funds amounting to one or two times its existing size, then the question must arise as to whether this is not something akin to a start-up. It may be one which has many aspects in its favour, such as an approved management team and stable operating systems, but it still has many of the risk associated with a start-up, not the least being that if it does not work there is nowhere to go, no escape routes via an existing business and these risks will be recognised in the costs associated with the funding. It will be more expensive to obtain equity funding for this type of project than for a true development capital project where the risks are comparatively lower.

(e) Management buy-outs

This is a form of financing which has grown rapidly during the last few years and has arisen where the management of an existing business form a consortium and buy the business from the owner. The company may well have been part of a large conglomerate or a family business where the family are no longer involved in the management. There are many occasions when this type of transaction can arise but the common theme is that the managers of the business acquire a stake in the ownership. There have been many reasons put forward why these have increased in activity, such as the reaction of large corporations that quickly grew by acquisition during the 1950s and 60s, then as the recession came in the 70s pressure was placed upon resources, cash being one of them, and it brought their focus of attention on to activities which were not in the mainstream operation and which could be sold to raise funds which could then be used to develop the areas that they decided to pursue long term. This may well be the case. It will be interesting to see if the downturn in the early 90s produces a similar upturn in management buy-outs shortly afterwards. I imagine that it probably will. Management buy-outs in the UK have been going for a long time although we only really began to call them that during the late 70s. The American marketplace has had a lot of experience in management buy-outs and although it is cyclical it does appear to have had an established level of activity.

There are now several variations on the same theme. The first is the straightforward management buy-out where the management obtain funding to buy the company and end up with a controlling interest in the business. Some of these transactions have been funded purely by loans and the management have obtained 100 per cent of the equity. This was more common a few years ago when sellers of companies to management were less certain as to the price they could expect and most deals were concluded at a discount to net assets. It was then possible to use these assets as security for loans after taking the appropriate action to ensure that the Companies Act was complied with. Often there was a real discounted value in the assets being purchased with the result that the level of borrowings could be relatively high, given an adequate level of stable profitability.

With the rise in awareness of what could be achieved in management buy-out situations occasioned not least by the high profile given to the activity by the financial press and the success of several large transactions, the prices that have been sought for management buy-outs by recent sellers have meant that it is now almost impossible to fund these purely by debt. There has to be a degree of investment in equity in most funding packages. This really then determines how much it becomes a management buy-out, or an institutional buy-out, where the institutions end up with a controlling interest in the company but are in effect backing the management who now have a minority stake. It is quite common now where this level of equity involvement is required by institutions, for the management to start with a low stake but have the ability to increase this quite often to the level of having control of the business by their performance over a period of several years. This can be achieved by a system of averaging profitability and the achievement of certain targets, such as redemption of preference share, all of which are specified at the outset. These can then be set against an agreed sliding scale and can provide a useful incentive working to both the institution's and the management's benefit.

There is a third variation on this which has seen more prominence in the US rather than the UK until just recently, and that is the 'leveraged buy-out'. In this situation a quoted company is bid for by a management team with institutional support. It is then taken private and the assets of the business used to secure a high level of debt. The rationale is that part of the business can be sold off to reduce the debt and the remaining activities re-organised or reduced and the new business then re-floated after this has been carried out. The amounts of money involved in these types of transactions are substantial and the management end up with only a very small stake and a high incentive package geared to make them produce results. Nevertheless, because of the sums of money involved, even a very small percentage of these types of businesses, if successful, can be very significant in terms of personal wealth. The level of activity in this area of leveraged buy-outs has been substantial with the result that prices and borrowings have been forced to extremely high levels. This has created vulnerability to rises in interest rates and recent failures in the US of highly leveraged corporations have brought severe criticism for the institutions which structured the deals. Here, as in everything else, an appreciation of risk and value is essential.

The underlying logic behind all these transactions, management buy-outs, institutional buy-outs, leveraged buy-outs, is that there is under-utilisation of resources at present and someone can see how these can better be put to use. The theory is that the management of the company controlled by shareholders removed from the business are often constrained in the action they can take to develop their own business, because they have to conform to large company budgets, or the family are unwilling to subscribe further equity or allow anyone else to do so and see their position diluted. If supported by independent shareholders who only wish to see the business prosper and who would support the management team, then a high level of profitability could be achieved and often assets which were surplus to requirements realised for cash. This is often proved to be true and there is a very low rate of failure in management buy-outs. One of the attractions from an institutional viewpoint is that the business, the management team and the products do not change. All that changes is ownership. Therefore the actual risk to the business arising from the transaction appears to be very low. With the company controlled by uninvolved family shareholders, this can quite often be true but with part of a large conglomerate undertaking the change it can be a very different operation. The first obvious point is how easily the company being bought out can exist without the group it was part of. Does it rely upon them for accounting controls and information? Are they in any way directly involved in the management? Are there any inter-company sales and will these continue? All these are questions which need to be asked and which will have to be checked upon and take a great deal of time and diligence. Most management teams will normally give straightforward answers to these points but the control systems employed by large groups are often very sophisticated and their management input is not always in a direct manner. By this I mean that despite protestations to the contrary, very rarely is a subsidiary in a large corporate entity left to go its own way and one of the greatest difficulties that I see management teams in new management buy-outs wrestle with is the transition from employee to principal. When the end of the week came and there was a problem, in the end it was a problem for the group and someone in the group was on hand to talk about it. After the buy-out there is no one and the management team stand or fall by their own decisions without recourse to anyone. This is a very difficult concept to convey to management teams that have spent a great amount of time within a large group and therefore have not necessarily always been subjected to this particular pressure. It is real, nevertheless, and can be a considerable strain on the team. With family businesses this can be less of a problem if the family really are removed solely into shareholder position, because a management team then has a much higher profile in terms of their decisions.

(f) Management buy-ins

This is a slight variation on the previous theme in that it still involves institutions backing a management team but in this case the management team does not come from within the business being purchased. The result of this must be that the risks are much greater — the management team have not operated together within the business being purchased and quite often they have not operated together completely before. It is unlikely that the senior key personnel will not have been working together but quite often they will have augmented the team with people they have identified as competent but not with whom they have been working directly. Again the logic is that the management team being backed identified a situation where there is an inefficient use of assets in an activity in which they have a demonstrable track record of success. It then falls upon them to convince institutions that this is a situation worth funding to allow them to undertake what is often fairly drastic action. It is quite likely that the business will be loss-making. Therefore there will be a very limited time to undertake remedial action and achieve a profitable situation. It is a proposition which commonly has a higher risk associated with it than a management buy-out because one would expect that a management buy-out should already be profitable when central administrative costs and group charges are removed whereas this type of operation depends upon someone else not making as good a job of running the business as a new management team and the bigger the mistakes that are being made the more likely it is that a business can be purchased. On the other hand, the larger the mistakes the more drastic is the remedial action required.

(g) Money out deals

A money out transaction should have its risk profile right at the far end of the equity capital spectrum of risk. By definition it should be on the level of risk that is even lower than that of a management buy-out. This type of transaction occurs when a minority shareholder in an unquoted company wishes to sell his holding. Quite often this arises through the death of a director and the family need to raise money to pay capital transfer tax, but it can be for various other reasons such as retirement of an executive director who wishes to raise some money from his shareholding now that he no longer will be involved in running the business and who wishes to have a liquid form of investment. It can also arise in a family company where members of the family who have not directly involved themselves in the business need to raise money for personal reasons, and where their largest asset is a shareholding in a private company which in itself is extremely illiquid. This can often cause a problem for the existing management who cannot necessarily raise the funds required to buy the shareholding personally and even with the change in legislation enabling a company to buy its own shares they may not consider it a prudent course of action if they can envisage the company utilising those resources at some later stage in its development. The alternative then is to find a third party to buy the shares. This is where it can be advantageous to seek the assistance of an institution to purchase these shares rather than an arbitrary third party. Institutions can be good partners in this type of operation because they have clearly defined objectives and it is possible with a little training to anticipate how they will react in a given set of circumstances. When an institution enters into an unquoted equity transaction it looks for the possibility of an exit, normally involving a sale or a flotation, fairly quickly. With a money out deal an exit may not be as obvious as with other transactions. Therefore there will be some form of compensation for lack of liquidity, normally a high running yield via a preference dividend. This allows the institution to remain in the investment, covering its funding costs and making a small profit without having to rely on a large capital gain being achieved at some indeterminate time in the future. For this to occur the company in which the institution buys shares needs to possess certain characteristics. Firstly, it needs to be able to demonstrate a stable, growing profits trend and be in an established position in its business. It does not need to exhibit the level of growth normally associated with capital gain type transactions but it does need to be capable of achieving real growth each year and of paying a regular dividend several times covered by profits.

4 Conventional bank finance

The fundamentals when viewing either a banking or an equity investment transaction are the same. The only difference is where the area of risk lies for the investor or lender. With the equity transactions we have just considered there is an implicit understanding that the investor cannot succeed unless the company succeeds and if the company loses he loses also. Equity finance is about creating change. The introduction of money into a business must create a situation where the business is being encouraged to do something that it has never done before. This must also bring with it all the risks associated with change, one of which must be failure. Looking across the spectrum of equity transactions, it can be seen that at the beginning money is being invested in a start-up and changes are occurring on every front there is. Consequently the risks are very high. As we move through to management buy-outs there is a very small element of change in the trading activities of the business until in a money out deal the money is not being introduced into the business at all. Instead it is going to an existing shareholder and the only change is change in ownership of the shares. There should be no impact at all on the business except the requirement to pay dividends. Nevertheless, in all these transactions the risk is that if the trading of the business fails there is little opportunity to receive anything back. You are last in line standing behind every other creditor the business has. With conventional bank finance it is still fairly critical that the fundamentals of the business are right to allow trading to progress, but if the business fails then it is not anticipated that this will result in loss of funds by the bank. Why should it? The bank is not taking any share in the profit if it is successful; why should it take a share of the losses if it fails? The result is that the bank views its areas of risk differently to an equity investor and value of security obviously features highly after trading considerations. At best, projections are an anticipated outcome and the longer the bank is committed to a specific level of exposure the higher its risk is because less reliance can be placed upon projections and more reliance has to be placed upon security. Consequently, the quality of security that is perfectly acceptable for a short-term transaction, for example, a charge over stock and debtors, may not be adequate for the bank to feel comfortable to make available a term loan at the same level for, say, five years. This is a point which quite often causes confusion in borrowers. Secondly, although lending unsecured is viewed as a higher risk than secured for the same company, from company to company it is not necessarily so and an unsecured loan to a large company may well be regarded as a better risk than that of a secured long-term loan to a small company. This goes back to stability of earnings, ability to withstand shocks and an estimate of the worth of the balance sheet upon liquidation. Gearing levels of large companies are often lower than those of smaller companies and the bank may well hold the view that there would be inadequate dividend declared for unsecured creditors (not equity holders) in the event of a liquidation.

In summary, the levels at which banks will make available facilities independently of the quality of the earnings of a company may be viewed as related to time and security.

Types of financial instruments

For the sake of clarity, this is an appropriate point to mention the more common financial instruments, bearing in mind that although they have a degree of risk inherent in their construction, the circumstance in which they are used is more likely to determine the overall risk attaching to them. For example, an overdraft could be used to finance a situation that was really an equity risk when looked at from fundamentals. The fact that an overdraft is being used would not make it less of an equity risk and if the institution concerned was not taking an appropriate reward then if this was a common attitude for it to take its return on funds invested would begin to look very weak over a period of time. From the company's point of view, it could be regarded as having succeeded if it achieved equity funding without having parted with any equity but, as has been mentioned earlier, that would be true if everything went according to plan, but if things went badly it could have unwittingly increased the risks it was running and this could result in the failure of the business completely.

I have set out the various products in order of short, medium and long term with a brief description attaching purely for the sake of clarification when confronted by these in following chapters. It is not a comprehensive description.

Short term

Overdraft A short-term facility, normally repayable on demand, with interest charged on a daily basis. For this reason it is probably one of the most efficient ways of borrowing money for a fluctuating requirement. An overall limit is set by the bank and drawings can be made against this normally by use of a cheque book. Interest rates are usually linked to the bank's published base rate although occasionally it is possible to link it to some other determining rate.

Money market lines These are the closest equivalent of overdrafts but the bank borrows the money in the inter-bank market in London for specific fixtures ranging from one day to one year. The money therefore has to be taken in specific tranches for designated periods and the interest rate is a margin over LIBOR, which stands for London Inter-Bank Offered Rate, and is the rate over which the bank can buy funds in the inter-bank market. It does not have quite the same flexibility as an overdraft and minimum tranches of around £25,000 are normally required. Unless overnight drawings are always made there will be the need to borrow slightly more than will be required to allow a contingency factor.

Acceptance credit facility This is an arrangement which allows the company to borrow money for periods of up to 30, 60 or 90 days in the London Bill Market. The bill is essentially to finance trade and therefore has to be drawn up in a way indicating that it is doing this. The bank then adds its signature to the back of the bill thereby assuming liability for the debt. This is known as acceptance by the bank and the signature of the bank enables the bill to command the finest rates in the market place known as Eligible Bill Rate. The bank can either arrange for the bill to be sold in the market or to buy the bill itself, perhaps to hold until maturity and credit the customer's account with the difference between the sale proceeds and the fee it charges for accepting the bill.

Short-term guarantees These often relate to import guarantees such as guarantees for VAT payments on imports and other customs duties. The guarantee allows the goods to be released from the warehouse and sold thereby generating sufficient funds to enable payment of all duties etc. A bank would normally regard a short-term guarantee as the same risk as an overdraft and merely allocate part of the overdraft facility to accommodate it. For a longer term guarantee a slightly different approach is taken.

Foreign exchange lines This facility enables the company to purchase, through its bank, either spot (at that time) or future foreign exchange contracts. These can be for up to two years' delivery depending on the depth of market in any particular currency. From the bank's point of view this is not quite the same exposure as lending the company the money because if the company has asked the bank to buy dollars for three months forward the bank is not going to release the dollars in three months' time until the company has paid for these funds. If the company defaults, the bank still has the dollars and the costs are those of reversing the transaction. These would be mainly transaction costs and the exchange movement of sterling against the dollar over the last three months. In practice banks tend to take the view that the exposure to a transaction of this nature is between 20 per cent and 30 per cent of the total transaction and would allocate an appropriate part of the overdraft facility to cover it if one existed.

Letters of credit This device is used to sell or buy goods from overseas companies without having to concern yourself with whether they can pay or you can convince them that you can pay. It is an undertaking given by your bank to another bank, or the reverse, that upon presentation of certain shipping documents relating to a specific transaction then your bank can advance you funds in the knowledge that it will be paid by the purchaser's bank. There are various operating costs associated with a letter of credit and in particular how many times it is used in one contract. However, if you ask your bank to open a letter of credit in favour of an overseas supplier, then they will look upon that as an irrevocable undertaking to pay and view it as if they had lent you the money. Therefore the exposure will be regarded as equal to part of the overdraft's facility although only a margin, eg 2 per cent, will be charged for the commitment as at that stage it is more in the nature of a guarantee because the bank does not actually have to supply the funds. The minute the bank pays the supplier's bank under the letter of credit it will debit your account correspondingly and it will then become part of your borrowing from the bank under the overdraft facility and be charged accordingly.

Medium term

Medium-term loans These loans are not repayable on demand as with an overdraft facility. Instead they represent a medium-term commitment by the bank, normally between three and five years, and have what is called a structured repayment, that is, at pre-determined intervals the loan will be reduced by an agreed amount. Sometimes it is not until the end of the term that the whole repayment is made, in which case the loan is often referred to as a 'bullet' repayment schedule. It is important to understand that this type of facility is an undertaking by the bank to provide money for that period and it cannot ask for its money back earlier unless there is some event that occurs that breaches the undertaking of the borrower. Such an event may be non-payment of interest or not making a repayment when due. It could be breaching one of the covenants which are incorporated in the loan, ie the company might have allowed its borrowings to exceed a specific figure or allowed another bank to take security when all lenders are supposed to be unsecured. On the other hand, the borrower quite often has the right to early repayment if he wishes although this is sometimes accompanied by the payment of a fee called a 'pre-payment fee', eg 1 per cent of the amount prepaid if repayment occurs in the early years of the facility. This is taken in part to compensate the bank for having undertaken a contract for five years but only received a proportion of the remuneration that would have arisen if the loan had run its course.

Interest rates can be fixed or variable. If variable they are more likely to be related to LIBOR and they will have specific interest fixtures such as three or six months which would represent the periods that the money has been borrowed from the inter-bank market. The advantage that a term loan has for a company is that it is an amount of borrowings in the balance sheet which has a degree of permanence about it. The borrowings do not have to be repaid tomorrow and therefore allow longer-term projects to be funded on a basis which is more in line with the anticipated earnings flow.

Performance guarantees I have included these in medium-term commitments but they can be for any length of time, depending upon the contract that they are attached to, and quite often there is a whole series of bonds attaching to one contract with quite different reduction profiles. I have set out below a theoretical list of contract guarantees or bonds as they are sometimes called. One of my legal colleagues has always informed me that strictly these instruments should be called guarantees if there is a sum of money involved, ie a sum of money is being paid over and the guarantee states that if certain events do not happen that money will be returned. Otherwise, if it is just an undertaking to pay under certain circumstances without having received any money, it should be regarded as a bond. Although these requirements are quite common within the UK, they really came into prominence when there were large amounts of construction work being undertaken in the Middle East and the size of bonds being requested to support large contracts were such that they had to be syndicated between several banks.

Bid bond This is an undertaking given by a bank that is submitted at the same time as the bid or tender goes in (it is often referred to as a tender bond). The purpose of having this undertaking is to ensure a degree of commitment on the part of tenderers to carry out what the tender has indicated. This arose, I suspect, from firms submitting tenders with prices in them which they tried to re-negotiate before signing a contract. A bid bond is normally for around 5 per cent of the contract price and lasts either until the contract has been awarded or for a period of 90 days. If a company does not enter into the contract having been awarded it on the basis of its tender, then the company requiring the contract can go to its bank and demand payment under the bid bond for the 5 per cent of the contract price.

Advance payment guarantee With large contracts it is often very expensive to set up a contract itself. Often large numbers of workers and machinery have to be moved into position (an advance payment is also referred to as a mobilisation payment) or work has to be undertaken on pre-fabricated units. Therefore to enable all this to happen the contracting company receives an advance payment. However, to ensure proper stewardship of these funds, it has to provide a bank undertaking that if certain events do not occur, then this advance payment will be returned. It is normally an amount of between 10 per cent and 20 per cent of the total contract and reduces against certificates from some relatively neutral body, such as a firm of consulting engineers or architects.

Performance bond This is an undertaking given at the start of the contract that the contract will be completed; if not, demand can be made under the bond. It is not normally for the full amount of the contract but quite often for, say, 30 per cent of it and it will reduce over the life of the contract against certified stages having been reached, so that at the end of the contract it should be zero.

Retention guarantee This is the reverse of a performance bond and increases throughout the life of the contract as stage payments are made. It is quite normal practice to hold back part of the stage payment and only make available, say, 90 per cent each time, holding back 10 per cent until the end of the contract when all these accumulated 10 per cents can be released against satisfactory acceptance on completion. A retention guarantee is given to allow the extra 10 per cent to be paid but to provide the payer with the comfort that he can call it back from the contractor should the contract not go according to plan.

Maintenance bond This is a bond given at the end of satisfactory completion of the contract when the contracting company undertakes to enter into a maintenance agreement for a certain period of years — say, five years. This bond is provided so that the maintenance contract will be carried out and performed in accordance with the terms of the contract. If it is not then demand can be made under the bond.

It is probably worthwhile pointing out at this stage that although most of these bonds are what are termed 'on demand bonds' — that is, no documentary evidence is required, it is merely sufficient for the bondholder to present himself at the appointed bank and demand payment — in fact there have been very few cases of unfair calling.

Banks have a tendency to regard bonds as if they were a term loan that they were providing although in these circumstances the overriding consideration is always the ability of the company to perform and there is not an initial repayment obligation. The difference between a term loan and a bond is that it is quite possible for a company to meet its obligations under a performance bond when undertaking a contract and thereby get released from it and yet make a loss on the contract, which in itself would have prevented the company from making repayment of a term loan. A bond does not require positive cash flow for its conditions to be met. There is some recognition of these facts in that banks generally allow a much higher level of bonding to be issued for a company than they would allow straight lending to be made available.

Convertible loan These are generally term loans which have been made available on something less than conventional banking terms. It might be that the security is weak, it could be that the rate is much lower than would have been anticipated in the market, or it could be that it is termed subordinated debt, ie it ranks behind certain creditors in a liquidation. In any event, it requires some extra element of reward to compensate the holder for having an inferior position and this reward is normally the ability to convert part of the loan into the equity of the company at a predetermined price. The price may well change over time but the change will be defined at the time that the holder subscribes for his stock. The advantages of a convertible loan stock from a holder's viewpoint are that it provides an income bearing security during the time to conversion and a higher priority in a liquidation than the equity holder. It also allows a judgment to be made about the company's later performance and if the conversion price does not look attractive when the time for conversion comes around, then the holder stays with the loan stock and the loan will have to be repaid as if it were a normal term loan. It gives the holder the opportunity to gamble a little lower income against the prospect of being able to convert into the equity at a price which is above the current market price but not at an unacceptable premium in view of the company's anticipated performance. From the company's viewpoint it allows equity to be raised at a higher price than would be currently possible but at the cost of the loan stock coupon. It works well when funds are required for a project which would have significant impact on the company's profitability but only in several years' time.

A variation on this is a loan stock with warrants. This is exactly the same except that the convertible element has a separate identity, called a warrant, which allows the holder to subscribe for shares at a certain price at a given time in the future. Initially a holder of loan stock would receive his loan stock together with a warrant but it is possible for the warrant and the loan stock to be sold separately and if it is a quoted stock two prices are made, one for the loan stock and one for the warrant.

Redeemable preference shares This particular instrument can be compared to a term loan except that it has a lower priority in liquidation. It is a share which does not participate in the equity of the business. It is only entitled to a fixed dividend (called a coupon) and because of this it normally pays a bit more than you would expect to pay for a term loan. It is redeemable, which means that the company undertakes at a specific point in time to buy in the shares at an agreed price, but the company can only do so if it has sufficient distributable reserves to allow this transaction to take place. It therefore has to have made sufficient profits in the intervening period. (Technically it could also be redeemed by another issue of shares and by using the proceeds to redeem the preference shares.) From the company's viewpoint it is a good instrument to have instead of a term loan because it is viewed as being included in shareholders' funds if the redemption period has long enough to run. Its main disadvantage is that it is more expensive. However, if the company has not generated sufficient profits to pay the dividend, then it is not obliged to make a payment. Similarly, it is not obliged to redeem the capital if it cannot do so, whereas with the term loan both of these events would give rise to circumstances termed default being declared and procedures being undertaken to recover the money. From the investor's viewpoint, unless the instrument is quoted it is not a very attractive instrument to hold. It really needs to be linked to some conversion terms into the equity of the company.

Long term

Loans They are the same as for medium-term loans except that they range from five to 15 years and because of this they are quite difficult to obtain. It is almost impossible for a bank to know what is going to happen in 15 years' time and therefore greater reliance will be placed upon security in these situations and a higher margin for error allowed, eg if a loan was being made against a 75 per cent valuation of a property for a medium-term loan this may well only be 60 per cent for a long-term loan. There could be clauses which allow for the bank to insist that the security was topped up if it fell below a certain value, but most banks do not want to enter into situations where they know they will have to ask for security to be topped up. Instead they prefer to start with a lower value at the outset.

Convertible loans The conditions applying to these are exactly the same as for the other convertible loans except that there is a longer period for conversion and therefore there is a greater chance for the share price to rise above the exercise price of the conversion terms. In other words, the company has longer to get it right. However, set against that is the fact that the holder is locked into a low interest bearing security because repayment in the event of non-conversion will be very far away indeed.

Preference shares Unless a company is quoted and there is a market made in these instruments there is very little incentive for anyone to hold them, as they are irredeemable. Therefore the only chance of getting your money out is to sell them to someone else, which could be difficult. They are far less attractive than redeemable preference shares and consequently have to pay a higher coupon. Unless they are for a large quoted company they are generally only used when they have conversion rights into the equity of the company.

Ordinary shares These are the lowest point in priority in a liquidation. They rank after every other creditor. However, when the company prospers the holders of these instruments have attributed to them the profits which are left after payment of interest and preference dividends. They entitle the holder to vote at meetings of the company and represent a proportion of ownership of the business. It is possible to have various classes of ordinary shares and give each of them different class rights but in essence the underlying concept of ownership and equity participation remain.

As I mentioned earlier, the purpose of this chapter and discussion of the instruments mentioned in it is to give an idea of the purpose of the instrument, when it might be appropriate and also how the bank would view it.

Chapter 3

THE RISK REWARD RELATIONSHIP — LENDING

We have already dealt in some detail with the various types of financial transactions and the more common instruments that might be employed by an institution in structuring a proposal. What is next required is to understand how the institution itself views a request for finance. The next two chapters deal with the risk reward aspects of the two major facilities that are sought from banks and financial institutions, namely that of lending and that of equity investment. By explaining how an institution will view its risk reward relationship in these circumstances, it will enable a better understanding of why certain requirements attach to specific instruments and what is most probably going to be the result of any particular request for funding.

The bank's requirement to make a profit

This chapter is going to concentrate on the risk reward relationship that will attach to a conventional lending proposition, but before we get into any great detail let us consider where the bank starts from and what its overriding requirements will have to be. The bank may be public or private but the directors will have an obligation to their shareholders to produce a return on capital invested in the bank. Secondly, in the UK it can only act as a bank with the consent of the Bank of England so the requirements of the Bank of England in terms of day-to-day operations have also to be taken into consideration.

The starting point in viewing a bank's lending criteria, then, is its key objective to make a profit and the reason a bank needs to make a profit when undertaking banking business is: to provide a return to the shareholders, to reassure depositors who place money on deposit with the bank to earn a rate of interest which can only come through the bank investing that money prudently and, finally, to expand the capital base to facilitate growth and provide a cushion against any losses. It is necessary to understand that these criteria apply only to banks. Other institutions will have different criteria for achieving profit but we will deal with that when we consider the risk reward of equity investment.

The Bank of England's position

The Bank of England monitors the capital adequacy of banks in the UK as part of its overall responsibility for the supervision and maintenance of confidence in the banking system. Not all banks undertake the same type of business but it is important that all businesses operating as banks and taking deposits from the public maintain the confidence of the public to prevent a general withdrawal of funds from any one particular bank which would then work its way through the banking system and would create a very serious situation. In particular the Bank of England has emphasised two ratios on different sides of the bank's balance sheet. They are:

(a) Gearing — which is the ratio of capital resources (or broadly, shareholders' funds) to current liabilities (which approximate to deposits). If a bank wishes to increase its lending a limitation on gearing forces a bank either to return to its shareholders for funds or increase its profitability, which will be reflected in an increase in its capital resources allowing a higher level of borrowing (ie taking deposits) for further lending.
(b) Risk asset ratio — this is the ratio of capital resources to the sum of all the assets employed, eg loans, guarantees, etc. multiplied by a specific risk factor appropriate to each class of asset. A limitation on the risk asset ratio could prevent banks from undertaking high risk business unless they had adequate resources to absorb losses. A bank must ensure that the returns on each class of risk that it undertakes are adequate to cover the losses that will occur in that class. This is the basic principle of the risk reward relationship.

A quotation from one of the Bank of England's papers sums it up very well: 'A sufficient flow of earnings is essential as a first defence against losses and as a source of fresh capital to allow the business to grow.' Given these considerations we can now approach the reward that an institution will seek for lending.

Lending risk

When entering into the business of lending there are always two underlying risks — the first is that you will lose your capital, the second is that you will not get your interest paid. It is therefore perfectly logical that the banker should be preoccupied with the idea of protecting his capital and ensuring that a borrower generates adequate funds to pay interest on a regular basis. We have already touched upon the difference between lending and equity investment and it is a very important distinction and necessary to understand when asking a bank for money. First of all, this is because you may be talking to the wrong people who cannot supply the facility you really want and, secondly, because you will go in understanding that you will be asking someone to invest in your company as well as perhaps lend to it and the relationship with the institution in both cases is different. An investor is a true partner of the business and therefore needs a different degree of information. The lender is a supplier of financial resources to the business and very much on an arm's length basis. People asking for money very often expect banks to take risks as if they were something more than a supplier of services to the business. One amusing comment about bankers is that they are in the money rental business and this is seen to have some sort of derogatory undertones but to some extent it is true. One of the closest analogies of banking is the car rental business — both parties provide an asset for use for a specific period of time, both charge a rate based on time and both expect the asset to return to them in good condition. The difference is that the car rental company has title to the asset all the time it is in the customer's use and in the event of the liquidation of the business the asset is owned by the rental company. This is not so with the banker's assets — money cannot be identified in this way. Money is only useful if it moves into other people's hands. All a banker has is a promise from a person he has given it to that when the time comes he will try to give it back. If the company goes into liquidation in the meantime then that is too bad because there is no particular asset owned by the company which the banker can say is that he lent to the company. The banker will therefore try to assure himself that the company will be capable of repaying him on a going concern basis. This means that if the funds are lent to the company then on the basis of what the company has shown itself capable of achieving it should be capable of continuing to generate sufficient profitability and cash flow with an adequate margin contingency to take account of any uncertainties over an agreed period of time, ie the life of the loan, first of all to make interest payments and secondly to make capital repayments. This is the first step in all lending transactions, answering the question 'Can the business generate adequate cash flow to justify the amount of money that it is requesting?' The magnitude of the borrowing in relation to the size of the company and existing lending will determine how closely the company has to be reviewed. For example, if a profitable company with a stable track record and no existing borrowings was seeking to borrow 20 per cent of its shareholders' funds for three years, then if the business was presented as remaining stable the degree of research that would have to be done into the background of the company and its industry would be considerably less than if a company in a very volatile business with borrowings already at around 70 per cent of shareholders' funds was seeking to borrow up to 140 per cent. These are extreme examples but I think they serve to illustrate the point.

The criticism is often made of banks that they place too much reliance on historical information and I am sure in many cases that this is justified, but if you are seeking to assess how a company will perform in the future it would seem illogical not to take advantage of any existing information that was available about the company as that will show how the management team has performed, what their attitudes have been, what sorts of markets it has been experiencing and what stage the company has reached. A company's future is very strongly determined by its history. This does not mean that markets cannot change and that new technologies cannot be introduced. All it means is that in these circumstances it would be unwise to predict the future without investigating the past. This also does not mean to say that if you walk into a bank and say, 'I have been making profits of £50,000 a year until now. Lend me £20,000 and I will make £100,000 a year' you will get the same reception as if you had been making £80,000 a year. Profits that are going to be made are never given the same weighting as those that have already been made. This is equally true when valuing a company in terms of profitability. You would expect to pay a high multiple of earnings, say 10 times, for profits that have actually been achieved that year whereas for profits that were going to be achieved you would only expect to pay a multiple say of seven or eight times. So it is with banks; account will be taken of possible increased profit and cash flow for repayments of loans but they cannot form the basis of the transaction. You will note that I refer to cash flow all the time. This is because that is what will repay the loan, not profit, and therefore this is what will be the focal point of the bank. The bank will expect to see an average level of cash flow that enables it to feel confident that the company can continue to generate three or four times the annual interest charge. This figure is obviously a rule of thumb and the stability of earnings will vary from industry to industry. For example, a cyclical engineering company should probably have a higher interest cover than a property company with a high quality long-term rent portfolio. If the bank can be satisfied that under normal circumstances it will be repaid by the company it then has to consider what will happen if the normal circumstances do not come about as they were expected to do. As I mentioned earlier, one of the principal elements about lending is that the bank makes loans in the knowledge that if the company goes into liquidation it should still receive its money back. It therefore has at least two independent courses of action available which will repay its loan. This is not to say that in practice they always work. Banks do lose money but it is not the intention at the outset that there should only be one way to be repaid. The second course of action is often achieved by the taking of security in some form or other. It could be a fixed charge over some of the assets of the business — this is known as a mortgage. It could be a floating charge over all the assets of the business which are not specifically identified, until the charge is said to have crystallised, at which point all the assets in the business are caught by the charge and are available to repay the bank. It could also be a guarantee from another company that was considered capable of repaying the facility or perhaps a guarantee from the directors supported by charges on their assets. There are many ways of taking security but the aim is always the same, to ensure that the bank has another way of seeking repayment in the event of failure of the business to generate cash to repay the loan. Security itself has to have certain attributes to make it suitable for why it is being taken. These are fairly obvious factors when looked at independently but nevertheless they must be present. It first of all needs to be easily quantifiable, ie it can be easily valued. Secondly, it needs to be easily liquidated, which means that should it need to be sold there should be a ready market available. Thirdly, it needs to be capable of passing title easily, ie it should be possible for the bank to take title to the assets cheaply and without any form of contention.

Now that we have identified what the major considerations that a banker will be seeking are, we need to understand how he will react when confronted with a request for funding, and that answer should be logically. He will first of all go through the main aspects of the transaction and test them firstly against what he considers to be realistic and secondly against what he is willing to underwrite. The order that each institution takes with its checklist might not be the same but I am sure that all the items will be covered one way or another. They are as follows:

What are the funds to be used for?

To what purpose will they be put? This is a very important argument of the proposition because it is far more difficult to obtain funds for non-productive purposes, eg a company plane or upgrading boardrooms, than it is for productive use such as a new computer or another finishing line. Not surprisingly, people who lend money to a business would much prefer the funds to be spent on improving the business's capacity to generate profits than only improving its assets. It is also important to explain the purpose properly so that the final projections can be properly understood. For example, although the money may be spent on buying another lorry, there could be other requirements arising from this transaction such as existing staff or more working capital requirements and it would be necessary to explain and justify that these have been fully included in projections and the total requirement.

Company product

What business is the business in? Is it growing or contracting? What has happened during the last three or four years? How is the company now regarded in the business and by its competition? What is the competition? Is it possible that they too are undertaking substantial plans of expansion? What would be the effect on capacity if they followed similar plans? What would happen if they didn't follow similar plans? How strong is the customer's product position? What particular skills does he have which distinguish him from his competition — is it product, service, market position or is it price? Is the company known to the bank? If so, how is the management team regarded? If not, can references be taken upon them from other sources?

Company—financial

What does the company's financial position look like? Here the last three years' accounts are useful and these should be audited. Has the company achieved a good record of profitability? Also, how much of the money has been kept in the business and how much has been paid out to shareholders? How much do the directors take out of the business? Is their remuneration purely for managing the business or is part of it compensation for owning the business? What is the current level of borrowings? Are they seasonal requirements or do they remain fairly constant throughout the year? Are they constant throughout the month? How much of the funds employed in the business comes from outside, ie banks plus trade creditors, and how much comes from the shareholders? This gives a good idea of how highly geared the business is and how vulnerable it could be to a reduction in trade credit. A comparison of the current liabilities against current assets will give an overall indication of how liquid the business is but how easily it could turn those assets into cash will be given by adding together the figure of cash plus debtors. Then comparing this with current liabilities will give an indication of how many of the debtors could be met quickly if need be and how much stock would have to be converted into cash to repay them. The theory is that debtors will pay in due course and therefore they can be regarded as more liquid than stock which often has to be completed and then sold before it generates cash, and it could be some time before it all takes place. Other aspects of consideration which give an indication of the working of the business are how quickly the money is being collected and how much credit the company is taking from suppliers. These will give an idea of how the business is operating. It is also worth investigating the spread of customers and suppliers and how vulnerable the business is to the loss of any one particular customer or withdrawal of trade credit. These are all logical questions to ask and it is important that the conditions that have prevailed in the past are built into the projections for the future of the business. It is always possible to improve terms of trade but history shows that this is rarely achieved dramatically. Generally it is a gradual process and if projections do not show this for the near future then they immediately start off being regarded with suspicion by bankers.

Company — the management

Of all the headings this is the most critical because it is this group of people who will determine how the company will progress over the life of the loan. It is also the most subjective as it is very difficult to assess people except by the results they produce and the most obvious relevant results are manifested by the trading progress of the company over the last few years. However, this is not sufficient by itself as a more detailed understanding of the management's role and their strategy will be required. A company can produce good results by simply being in the right place at the right time and reacting to a demand for a product. It does not necessarily mean that it had a strategy for getting into that situation and that it has an agreed course of action for the future when demand for that particular product is not quite so high. A banker looks to see that the management team first of all have the necessary skills to undertake their executive responsibility and that these can be carried out in a formalised structure which allows the company to be controlled by the senior management. The second stage is to check that the senior management act as a team in determining strategy and that having done so they are then led by an identifiable member in achieving the goals that they have all agreed upon. It is extremely rare for a committee to be as successful in the day-to-day management of the business as a managing director is because it is not a format which allows fast decision-taking on an hour-by-hour basis. A committee is best suited to debating particular questions so that they receive measured consideration, such as strategy and questions of policy. The danger that a banker is looking for is either that the board has no leader or that the leader is so strong that the board cannot function as a board — it is just a puppet of the managing director.

The return

It was mentioned earlier that the need for profitable business motivated the banks to undertake lending and the reward that is sought is normally through a payment of interest. It sometimes may involve some fees but the bulk of the remuneration is from interest. The interest payment is normally expressed as a margin over cost of funds ie what the bank has to pay to obtain the funds or the opportunity cost of not investing them and it is this margin that the bank receives as its gross operating return.

The margin must therefore cover:

(1) The profit required on the deal

(2) A contribution to overheads

(3) A contribution to the bad debt reserve appropriate to the class of risk into which the asset falls.

The amount of profit that the bank is able to make on any particular transaction would be dependent upon several factors but probably the most significant of these will be competitive considerations. The financial market is a fairly efficient one and any large discrepancies are normally quickly eradicated.

If the requirement of (1) and (2) are ignored it can be seen that a margin on a loan of 3 per cent compared to 1 per cent on another indicates that the bank accepts that the former is three times more likely to fail than the latter. In order to break even on the 3 per cent risk class category assets, no more than one in every 33 equivalent loans should fail. It will be noticed that the ratio of margins to capital is such (ie 1:33) that a conventional lender would not undertake any business that would seem to have even a moderate risk of failing because the risk reward structure would not allow such a stance to be taken and for profits to be made.

We can now consider how, when the bank has identified a suitable lending opportunity, it sets about protecting its investment.

This protection is achieved through a document known as a loan agreement which can be as little as one page for loans of short duration but often runs to several pages when a loan is for a long period.

Protecting the lending investment

A loan will normally have conditions attaching to it, the breach of which will render it 'on demand'. Provided that these terms are not breached the loan will remain available for the contractually agreed term.

Many of these terms ensure that the borrower effectively remains within the risk class determined at the outset of the loan. A breach of a term therefore may not result in a demand for repayment but a renegotiation of the loan to re-structure the risk reward relationship, eg it could well result in an unsecured loan becoming a secured loan. What a bank is saying is that the loan was made on a certain understanding of the company's status. If this were to change then the bank would wish to have the right to reconsider the situation.

The loan agreement

This can be quite a daunting collection of paper when viewed for the first time but it is a logical collection of paragraphs when taken individually and these can normally be understood fairly easily. However, there is a tendency for legal phrases to creep into certain areas which can cause the layman to take a little longer to work it out.

The general outline of a loan agreement is as follows although the order may vary from institution to institution:

(1) Definitions

(2) Amount

(3) Purpose

(4) Availability

(5) Repayment

(6) Terms

(7) Security

(8) Covenants

(9) Negative covenants

(10) Default

(11) Pre-conditions

(12) Warrants

(13) Acceptance

It is useful to consider the contents and purpose of these paragraphs as they should be fully understood before any agreement is entered into. If you feel that any particular clause is too onerous or unacceptable to you then you should attempt to re-negotiate it before signing.

1 Definitions

The purpose of this paragraph is to ensure that there is no doubt later on in the document when certain items are referred to. In addition it can also be used to identify shortened forms of term, eg:

'the Bank'	XYZ Bank Limited
'the Company'	ABC Limited
'Financial Year'	An accounting reference period of the company under section 224 of the Companies Act 1985

2 Amount

This should state how much money will be made available and in what currencies. It could be an amount of, say, £500,000 which might also be capable of being drawn in sterling, dollars or deutschmark equivalents.

3 Purpose

The original discussions with the bank will have been to obtain money for a specific requirement and it is this which should be stated here, eg the loan should be utilised to acquire the issued share capital of LMN Limited. It could be that there are several purposes or that it is a very general application, eg working capital requirements.

4 Availability

Here the bank will state how the company may take the funds. It could be that the bank will require a short notice period before funds are made available to enable it to schedule its borrowing requirements in the inter-bank market.

This paragraph should also stipulate the size of tranches that the money can be borrowed in, eg multiples of £100,000, or perhaps in one amount equal to the principal amount of the loan as specified in (2) above.

It should also give an indication of how long a borrower has to draw down the facility after which time it is normal for any undrawn portions to be cancelled and repayments etc. to be reduced pro rata.

If the facility is what is known as revolving then the undrawn portion will not be cancelled but be available until a later date should it be required.

5 Repayment

Hopefully this is self-explanatory. It should state clearly what the obligations of the company are to repay the facility, in what amount, which currency and upon which date, eg eleven equal quarterly instalments of £20,000 each commencing on the first anniversary of drawdown and a final instalment of £50,000 on the fourth anniversary of drawdown.

It is common for any early repayments of the term loan to be applied in inverse order of maturity. This means that in the example given above if £70,000 were repaid after six months then this would be applied to the eleventh payment of £20,000 and the final payment of £50,000, not to the first £70,000 of repayments. Therefore the new repayment schedule would be ten equal quarterly repayments of £20,000, each commencing on the first anniversary of drawdown. It is often common for early repayments to attract a penalty and this will normally be specified in this paragraph, eg if the company prepays the loan before the first anniversary of drawdown the company shall pay to the bank commission calculated at a rate of 1 per cent on the amount repaid.

Similarly, if the bank has to borrow money in the money market for specific periods as defined in the loan agreement, eg 1, 2, 3, 6 or 12 months or even longer, at a given rate, if the loan is repaid in the middle of one of these periods then it could be expensive for the bank to break the contract and there would normally be a clause allowing the bank to reclaim any costs from the borrower should this occur, eg if the bank had borrowed money for three months at 12 per cent and the loan was repaid after one month. If in the intervening period rates had fallen so that the two month rate was at 10 per cent, then the bank would either have to break the three month contract with the party it had borrowed from and pay a penalty, ie 2 per cent for two months, or continue paying a rate of 12 per cent on the deposit despite the fact that it did not have a matching asset earning 12 per cent plus a margin.

6 Terms

This should include all payments to be made to the bank such as arrangement or syndication fees and also interest charges.

The interest charges may be a fixed figure, eg 12 per cent for the life of the loan, or it may be variable and be related to a market rate such as LIBOR or base rate. If it is linked to base rate it is normally calculated on a daily basis taking into account any changes in the base rate when they are announced. If it is LIBOR-linked a specific period will be chosen to borrow the funds at a given rate. The date on which these periods expire is know as a 'rollover date' when the funds are rolled over into another interest period. Interest will have to be paid at an agreed period or at the end of a rollover period, whichever the loan agreement states.

The second element of a variable rate loan would be the margin which is a percentage addition, eg 2 per cent; then the rate becomes LIBOR + 2 per cent together with a third element for sterling loans which is known as MLA (Mandatory Liquid Asset requirements). This is to take account of the Bank of England requirement for banks to hold a certain percentage of funds lent in specific liquid instruments, eg cash or gilt edged stock, and the cost to the bank of having to maintain these liquidity requirements is added on to the interest charge. MLAs are normally calculated quarterly and vary depending upon prevailing interest rates. As an indication they normally add around 1/8 per cent per annum to the interest costs.

The interest paragraph should also indicate where the company should make its interest payments and by what time to ensure that the bank is in receipt of funds on that particular day and does not lose a day's interest.

7 Security

This should identify precisely what form of security is required by the bank, eg first legal charge, and from which companies, when there are several in a group, and whether any guarantees are required and if so from whom. It may well be that security is being shared with other institutions in which case a priority agreement will need to be agreed between the institutions setting out how distribution of funds arising from any realisation of security will be distributed between them. Details of priority letters and charge forms are not normally attached; instead the wording 'in a form acceptable to the bank' is often used, which normally means the bank's standard forms. However, if you are depending on the rapid completion of a facility it is well to ensure that the bank has reached agreement with any other institutions that may be present as to the wording and sharing of security because these points have a habit of being overlooked until the last minute.

8 Covenants

These are undertakings given by the company that it will maintain certain ratios or provide certain information, the most common of which are shown below by way of example. It is not usual for every one of these covenants to be included in the same loan agreement:

(a) *Information:*

(i) Copies of audited accounts not later than three months after the financial year to which they relate

(ii) Management accounts for each month within two weeks of the end of the month to which they relate

(iii) Cash flows and profit and loss forecasts for the next financial year to be available not later than one month before the end of the then current financial year.

(b) *Balance sheet:*

(i) Borrowings of the company shall not at any time exceed net worth (this is a gearing restriction to ensure that borrowings do not exceed shareholders' funds)

(ii) Borrowings of the company shall not at any time exceed 70 per cent of the aggregate amount of stock and debtors (this type of covenant, linking borrowings to a fluctuating asset, is often used when a floating charge is in place and the assets are being looked to for value of the charge)

(iii) Shareholders' funds of the company shall not exceed 50 per cent of the aggregate of shareholders' funds plus current liabilities plus other liabilities. (This is called a leverage covenant and its purpose is to limit the amount of outside funds that can be raised by the business without obtaining further permanent capital. To a certain extent it guards against over-trading)

(iv) Current liabilities of the company shall not at any time exceed current assets. (This is to ensure that the company always stays liquid and has sufficient current assets to meet its current liabilities)

(v) No reduction in tangible net worth (this should normally increase each year and ensures that there is no erosion in shareholders' funds during the lifetime of the loan)

(c) *Profit and loss:*

(i) Interest shall be covered at least three times by profits before interest and tax

(ii) The average pre-tax profits for any two consecutive years shall be greater than zero. (This allows the company to make a loss in any one year)

It is desirable both from the borrower's and the lender's viewpoint that covenants should be defined in an unequivocal manner and that they can be easily calculated. It is little use having a highly sophisticated covenant that requires a two-week investigation by accountants to calculate the result. Whenever possible it is desirable to link covenants to published information such as management accounts.

9 Negative covenants

This is where a company undertakes not to allow a specific course of action to occur.

(a) Security:

(i) Create or permit to subsist any charge, mortgage, pledge, lien or other security upon its undertaking property assets or any part thereof. (This is often referred to as a 'negative pledge' and is always included in an unsecured loan agreement. Exceptions have to be specified in the loan agreement, eg existing charges or charges securing loans to the value of an agreed amount, often very small in relation to the company's assets)

(ii) Dispose of its business or assets. (To ensure that the company undertakes the same business during the life of the loan)

(iii) Sell assets or services to third parties other than on normal commercial terms. (This ensures that the assets of the business are not diluted by sales below market value)

(iv) Make any payments or distribution. (This ensures that the company retains profits)

10 Default

This specifies the events under which default occurs and the bank's obligation to maintain the facility is released.

The first conditions are breach of either the positive or negative covenants and non-payment of interest or capital when due. Other fairly usual events of default include:

- appointment of a receiver
- resolution for winding-up
- if any security becomes enforceable
- if any indebtedness becomes repayable prior to maturity or not repaid when due
- a change in voting control of the company

These cover such events as the failure of the company and the non-performance of the company under other facilities (often referred to as cross-default).

11 Pre-conditions

These can include anything which the bank considers essential to completing the transaction and without which it is not prepared to advance the funds, eg:

- completion of security
- satisfaction with valuations
- changes to Memorandum and Articles of Association (if necessary to allow the directors to take specific actions required under the loan agreement)
- completion of the loan agreement
- completion of the bank mandate
- sight of the Certificate of Incorporation
- no event of default having taken place

12 Warranties

These are undertakings given by the company at the time of signing the loan agreement and normally are continuing warranties deemed to be given at every rollover date. Examples are as follows:

- the company is empowered to enter into the loan agreement
- there are no restrictions upon its ability to grant security or give guarantees or if there are then signing of this agreement does not breach them
- by signing this agreement it will not result in a default or breach under any other agreement
- no material litigation is being undertaken or contemplated by the company
- the audited accounts of the company give a true and fair view of its business and its financial circumstances
- there have been no material adverse changes in the business since the date of the latest audited accounts
- all material facts relevant to a lender have been made available to the bank

13 Acceptance
This paragraph explains how the document should be completed. Normally there are two signed copies sent to the company by the bank, one of which will be retained by the company and the other signed and returned to the bank within a specified period, say three weeks, together with a certified copy of the board's resolution authorising acceptance.

Other elements are often included in a loan agreement such as specifying the country's laws which will apply to it, what might happen if there were a change in current legislation, how the borrower and lender should be deemed to communicate with each other and to which addresses correspondence will have to go.

In this chapter we have looked at the types of risks that a bank will regard as conventional lending propositions and why it will not undertake the same risks as those taken by people with capital in the business if it is only to receive a fixed reward.

The bank uses the loan agreement to protect its lending investment. Therefore it is important that this document is fully understood before it is signed. Most banks are willing to be flexible in their approach to documentation if there are good reasons to be so. Consequently it is worthwhile seeking to negotiate a satisfactory document which will not cause you problems in several years' time. It is also worthwhile seeking professional advice if you feel in doubt or the document is complex, but there should be nothing in any loan agreement that cannot be explained to you. It is worth remembering that there is no absolute right or wrong form of loan documentation—only loan documentation that could cause problems by being too restrictive on your business and documentation that is not. The finally agreed document is nearly always a result of compromise between borrower and lender.

Chapter 4

THE RISK REWARD RELATIONSHIP — EQUITY INVESTMENT

Institutional approach to equity risk

We are now going to consider the approach taken by an institution when reviewing a potential equity transaction. Such an institution could be a bank in which case the points made in Chapter 3 will apply equally to this type of investment. However, the institution could equally well be one of the following:

- Insurance company, pension funds etc.
- Specialised funds
- Development corporations, grants
- Private investors
- Industrial companies

1 Banks

A bank is constrained in its development capital activity by the same Bank of England criteria as it is in its lending activity and, because unquoted equity investments have a relatively higher risk asset weighting than loans, they are quite demanding in terms of the equity capital required by the bank to support the business. Similarly, a high level of write-offs as a result of a high risk investment stance could cause a need for further capital unless profits from existing investments begin to come through fairly quickly.

In terms of equity investment the bank will nearly always assess the project as having to be undertaken by funds which it has purchased in the money market and therefore there is a continuing requirement to fund the interest on these amounts.

2 Insurance companies, pensions funds etc.

These types of organisations have long-term capital growth requirements and a regular inflow of income from contributions to pension and insurance schemes. Development/venture capital can represent a very useful part of their portfolio although there are often restrictions as to the proportion of their portfolio that they can hold in unquoted investments, eg only 5 per cent perhaps. They do not have the same capital adequacy requirements as banks nor are they so income conscious because the money they are investing has not been borrowed. It is payment for policies that will not require distributing for many years hence. Consequently a high concentration on capital growth is possible.

3 Specialised funds

These may well be tax driven, such as business expansion scheme funds where the subscriber to the fund receives tax relief for the amount of his investment, or they could be dedicated funds such as venture capital or investments in a particular region or industry. Whichever, the fund normally does not have any income obligation to subscribers, many of whom would be high rate taxpayers and therefore would not wish substantial investment income which would be tax inefficient. Instead, they are driven by capital gain. This can either come from liquidation of the fund and sale of the investments or, if the fund is quoted, disposal of the shares. A fund normally does not have restrictions such as capital adequacy except those it sets itself in its offer document when it is seeking subscribers. However, in the long term it still has a requirement to perform by making profitable investments in growth companies if its subscribers are to achieve their capital gain. It is quite common for the investment managers of the fund to have incentive schemes linked to the performance of the fund payable upon realisation of investments.

4 Development corporations, grants etc.

These types of bodies may make development capital available but their rationale for doing so is rather more complex than private organisations. Their reasons for existing are generally to encourage, develop and nurture job creation in their particular geographic area and often they seek to achieve this by putting up 'soft' monies for industrial activities to prime the pump and encourage other development capital institutions to put their money in. This can be very attractive for a potential seeker of funds as these types of corporations are less interested in the commercial reward that might be available than they are in ensuring that the project is funded.

5 Private investors

These are less predictable than most institutions and have varying requirements depending upon their personal circumstances. They can contribute significantly in areas other than finance if they have the appropriate experience. However, it is important that you feel confident with them as partners in your business because they are liable to be more emotional than a financial institution which is in the business of making investments and accepts that things quite often do not go according to plan.

6 Industrial companies

Some large industrial companies do have specialised development capital activities and these have the advantage that there is a depth of management expertise that can be called upon if required. It should always be borne in mind that unless the organisation in question has an arm's length development capital operation with investments and disposals entirely within its own discretion, then the reason for this activity is generally to acquire the business if it turns out to be successful. This may well meet with your requirements; if so it can be a very attractive source of funds. If you have other aspirations then tread carefully and make sure that you fully understand what it is that the organisation wishes to achieve by making an investment in your company.

It is important that when an institution is approached it is understood what its investment criteria are and it is also worth enquiring what the possibility of further financing is. Certain institutions may well not have the ability to follow their first investment because they are limited by size of fund and say they can only invest 10 per cent of their fund in any one area or it could be that by having one particular type of investor it rules out the possibility of having further financings provided by different types of institutions. There is no right institution, only the one that allows your company to achieve its objectives without incurring undue limitations.

Equity investment risk

When undertaking unquoted equity investment the overall risk is that the investment loses value. This might occur in two particular areas — on a going concern basis or upon a winding-up. On a going concern basis this could actually be worse than the company having to appoint a receiver. What happens is that the company's performance is poor but not sufficiently poor that a receiver has to be appointed. Instead it has to struggle on but it does not generate sufficient profits to pay a dividend and its performance is so unattractive that the investment cannot be realised. It becomes what is known in the US as one of the 'living dead'. It generates no income but it takes management time to monitor. When a company fails and a receiver is appointed, share capital ranks after all creditors in payments under a winding-up and if there are insufficient funds left after everybody else has been paid then the equity investor begins to lose the value of his investment.

An equity investor is less concerned with the protection of capital than a conventional lender because his approach accepts that a certain proportion of investments are going to fail and will have to be written off. What he is concerned to ensure is that the company in which he has invested has the odds sufficiently weighted in its favour that it can achieve a substantial increase in value whilst seeking a situation where the downside is limited. One of the ways of limiting downside is by seeking a company to invest in which has a relatively high net asset value per share and which is represented by tangible assets. By this is meant that if all the assets in the business were realised and used to meet the obligations of the business at that date, then if they were realised at book value the surplus available to shareholders would be equal to shareholders' funds, a figure often referred to as net asset value. It follows therefore that if a figure is paid for a company's shares in excess of net asset value per share, then upon a liquidation of its assets at book value the shareholders would suffer a loss equal to the difference between the price paid for the shares and net asset value per share. This is all well and good but it is complicated by the fact that the value of assets in the books of a company often bears no relation to their realisable value. To seek to protect an investment by using this approach an investor needs to go for assets that have a clearly defined value and which may be understated in the books of the company.

Another method of reducing the downside is by utilising a tax advantage such as the business expansion scheme whereby tax relief is received upon the value of the investment, effectively enabling the investor to calculate his exposure at a lower level than a straight investment would require.

These are all entirely sensible approaches but if an investor shows undue concern over the downside protection I would suggest that another institution is sought because successful equity investors become so by undertaking investments in successful companies, not by limiting risk in unsuccessful ones. An over-cautious investor is not going to produce the transaction that allows a business to achieve its full potential because he will lack the ability to back the management. Instead he will be trying to control their actions completely.

Reward

The reward that is sought by an equity investor can be received in two forms, either dividend yield or capital gain. The dividend yield is an important consideration when undertaking equity investment because it allows an investor to receive a running yield on his investment which is related to the performance of the company. Equally, if the company does not achieve profits then dividend payments are severely restricted, if possible at all. It is always a fine balance when structuring a transaction as to what sort of yield it should produce and what level of capital growth should be aimed at. Most equity transactions rely fairly heavily upon capital gain and this can be achieved by flotation of the company on a recognised market such as the USM, the capital gain being achieved because the company will be valued on a multiple of its earnings, after tax and preference dividends, known as a price earnings ratio, and hopefully the company will have grown since the institution involved invested in the company; and secondly, a quoted company attracts a much higher level of price earnings ratio than an unquoted one because its shares are liquid. This means that they can be easily bought and sold and therefore an investor is willing to pay for this particular attribute.

Another way that a realisation can occur is through a trade sale of the business and it can be seen that if an institution is relying heavily upon any particular course of action it will wish to assure itself that the management also contemplate going down this route. Similarly the management need to understand what the institution expects from them before they enter into an agreement together because it may well be that the management team does not want to go public or does not contemplate selling the business. This needs to be understood by all concerned at a very early stage because exits are important to institutions.

Pricing

This is a very subjective area but there seems to be a general market view that the return aimed for on unquoted equity investments is somewhere around 30 to 40 per cent p.a. at present. In practice this does not mean to say that it is always achieved but deals tend to be structured with this in mind. How this figure is achieved can vary. Banks have a tendency to require some dividend yield from their investments if they are capable of paying it. This can be quite attractive in that the higher the dividend yield on a running basis then the lower capital gain it is necessary to achieve when the time comes for realisation. A dividend yield is quite an attractive form of receipt for an institution because it is what is known as franked investment income, which means that it is not taxable in the hands of the company. Therefore it is equivalent to a payment after tax to the company as if it has borne tax at the company's current rate. However, as has been mentioned previously, not all institutions are funded in the same way and therefore some institutions may well not see dividend yield as a particularly attractive way of taking their remuneration, particularly if they do not suffer a high level of tax.

Protecting the investment

When undertaking equity investment the bank or institution seeks to exercise control over the company in which it is investing to ensure that the company cannot change its circumstances significantly without the approval of the external shareholder. The reason for this is fairly straightforward. The institution is quite often the only external shareholder and only has a minority position. All other shareholders are involved in the business. In these circumstances it is relatively easy, should it be desired, to ensure that the institution receives no dividend. Remuneration can be taken by other shareholders through other forms such as income and there might be very little incentive to provide the institution with an opportunity to realise its investment. If the institution knew that these circumstances would come about then it certainly would not have made the investment but now that it has done so there is very little that it can do to ensure that the original representations which were made to induce it to invest are adhered to. To allow the bank or institution to prevent such a set of circumstances occurring it takes certain rights and conditions when making an unquoted equity investment and these are normally contained in a document called the shareholders agreement. Sometimes some of the conditions are placed in the Memorandum and Articles of Association but as these are public documents and available to anyone for inspection who cares to look it is normally desirable to incorporate these conditions in an agreement which is the property of the company and does not have to be disclosed. It also has the advantage that if there are any changes to the agreement then it requires the consent of all parties but does not have to be done so publicly.

A typical shareholders agreement might include the following headings:

- Right to information
- Right to appoint a director
- Veto over certain management actions
- Right to be consulted over major changes in policy
- Voting control
- Borrowing powers
- Limitation of remuneration
- Pre-emption rights

As with covenants in a loan agreement, the purpose of these is to ensure that a certain course of action is followed except where shareholders have agreed to the contrary. If it is required to negotiate away any of these conditions as being unreasonable then the onus is upon the existing shareholders to give examples of circumstances where such covenants would appear to be restrictive or hinder rather than control the business. An institution generally feels very vulnerable with a minority position in unquoted shares and the facts of life are that they are backing the management to carry out a particular agreed plan and they are probably providing almost all of the finance required to achieve this. In these circumstances there is very little to prevent the management doing whatever they please with the new funds as long as the management control more than 51 per cent of the voting shares.

The shareholders agreement

There will, of course, be the usual items such as definition of terms used and a description of the circumstances which give rise to the transaction but the major elements are as follows:

1 Right to information

This is a very general clause and will include not just the items requested under the loan agreement covenants, ie accounts and management accounts within a specified period together with budgets etc., but also copies of all documents sent to the holders of any class of share at the same time as it is sent and details of all information made available to the board of the company or any of the boards of subsidiary companies. In other words, the institution wishes to be able to receive at the same time that it is relevant all pertinent information relating to the affairs of the company so that it is as well-informed as its co-investors who are running the business. In practice this should not result in the bank trying to run the business nor should it produce an onerous burden upon the financial systems. If it is felt that it does then you would be advised to discuss this matter in some detail with the bank or institution so that you understand precisely how they envisage operating. As I have noted before, it is not generally a good idea to enter into a situation, unless you have no alternative, where you are prevented from running your business on a day-to-day basis. However, this should not be confused with the need to keep co-investors informed. This can often be a new responsibility for a company when all shareholders have previously been involved in the business and therefore knew what was going on and it needs to be recognised there is a duty of stewardship by the directors for the funds which the bank has invested in the business; and if you are prepared to accept the investment you should also be prepared to set time aside to explain how the business is progressing and what the views of the board are for its prospects in the future.

2 Right to appoint a director

The right to appoint a director is very closely aligned to the right to have information. It should be remembered that an unquoted company does not have to undertake to make information available as a quoted company has an obligation to do and therefore the appointment of a director can be a practical way of ensuring that the institution receives the information it requires. Institutions vary in their exercising of this clause. Most take the right when making investments totalling in excess of £200,000 but some do not want the high visibility of being on the board of investments in case a failure occurs and creditors try to pursue their claims through to shareholders who obviously represent a more attractive proposition than a bankrupt company. This is not a very likely course of events and quite often a director is not appointed because the institution is quite satisfied with the information it is receiving and sees no reason to involve the company in further costs for non-executive directors. If the institution is capable of providing specialists from within its own organisation then it can be extremely beneficial to have the institutional director on the board because if he has been selected wisely he can contribute in areas where the company itself is weak. This can be achieved also by the institution appointing a non-executive director from outside who has a particular skill which he is able to bring to bear on the company's problems.

The occasions when institutions nearly always do insist on a non-executive appointment are, firstly, when there are several of them as a result of a syndication and therefore this represents a manageable way of all the institutions being represented without making the board unwieldy.

The other occasion is when there is a substantial sum of money being invested in the company and the institution considers it significant enough to warrant a board appointment. A board representative should not be viewed as a negative element in the transaction. It can be used very much to the company's advantage because it gives another dimension to the views being expressed around the boardroom table and it can serve as a good discipline in board meetings to have a non-executive present. The board meeting will be the main point of contact for the non-executive with the company and it ensures that it is held regularly and that elements which can easily be glossed over have to be explained and examined in commonsense terms.

It is also quite common for institutions to take the right to appoint the chairman of the company. This also should not be seen as a vote of no confidence in the management. Rather it should be regarded as a willingness to ensure that a company receives the support it requires. It is not uncommon in small companies for the post of chairman either not to be filled or alternatively not to be carried out effectively if the managing director is undertaking this role as well. An example of this can be at board meetings when the board are expected to express views as equals. If the managing director is attempting to chair the meeting and ensure that each argument receives an airing while at the same time ensure that his views are equally argued, he has considerable conflict of interest which can very easily result in him either overstating his views or failing to give them sufficient discussion. A non-executive chairman who has been employed perhaps in a larger organisation can make a very great contribution to board meetings as long as the personalities involved do not clash. This is a point to be discussed with the institution and it is essential to insist that when selecting clients for these types of posts there is a joint selection committee involving both institution and management. This goes some way to preventing the unfortunate mistakes the risks of which are inherent in all staff appointments.

3 Veto over certain management actions

The purpose of this clause is the natural consequence of the previous two. It can be readily understood that there is little point knowing about circumstances which for various reasons are unacceptable if there is no course of action which can be taken to rectify them. Unlike a loan, an investment in shares in an unquoted company is extremely illiquid and if circumstances arise which are contrary to the wishes of the shareholder it is extremely difficult to liquidate the shareholding. The directors of a company have powers defined in the company's Memorandum and Articles of Association and normally these are very widely drawn because it is impossible to forecast what a director will need to be able to do when a company starts trading. What an institution is seeking to do with these types of vetoes is not to prevent decisions being made but to ensure that they have to be consulted before they are undertaken. Nevertheless, a veto is precisely what it is and if the institution does not like a proposal it can stop it. This is a serious and powerful right and there should not be a whole string of vetoes in a shareholders' agreement. They should be capable of being justified by the institution both in terms of why they are included and the level at which they have been pitched. This is inevitably subjective to some extent but they must relate directly to any budgets and projections and must allow a considerable contingency before they begin to bite. A common example is a veto on capital expenditure above a certain level in any one year. This can be understood fairly easily in that if a company has put forward financial projections that indicate capital expenditure over the next five years will average £50,000 p.a. and a profit level of £150,000 p.a., it would be a matter of some concern if the board invested more than £75/100,000 in any one year. If they did so either they would have undertaken a new course of investment strategy or they would have budgeted very inaccurately. Whichever is the case, this is bound to have a severe impact on cash flow and borrowing requirements and these need to be fully discussed and reviewed before any decision of this nature is made. It is sometimes a useful technique to limit these vetoes to a percentage variance from budgets and these budgets will have been agreed by the board and the shareholders. Whatever the technique decided upon the important thing is that they are pitched at values which do not prevent the management from running the business and only you can decide whether this is the case or not.

In some ways these rights of veto are less onerous than covenants in a loan agreement because a breach in a loan covenant will result in a request for the money to be repaid whereas a request for a course of action for which the institution has a veto cannot result in the funds being returned to the institution. In addition, the institution will have every incentive in agreeing to it if they can be sure it is in the company's best interests because normally they will be locked into their shareholding.

4 Right to be consulted over major changes in policy

As a shareholder in the business the bank will wish to be consulted over any significant changes that might be made in the strategy of the business. This again is not because the bank objects to significant changes in policy but because it was induced to make an investment on the basis of certain representations about the policy of the company and the strategy of its management. No strategy should be adhered to blindly. It should always be questioned and reviewed in the light of current market conditions and anticipated developments. However, if a business wished to dispose of a subsidiary which accounted for, say, 20 per cent of its profitability and then used the proceeds to develop another product area, then this type of action is one where the bank would wish to be consulted. In practice there are very few substantial policy changes in businesses and when there are it is generally an occasion when the company involved wishes to seek the bank's views not just from the aspect of obtaining approval but as another party who will have a contribution to make and who, as they will not be involved in the day-to-day running of the business, will not have the same emotions about the various marketplaces and activities. This particular clause is normally drafted in a fairly general way because it is difficult to be specific about what precisely constitutes a major change in policy before it occurs and therefore it depends very much upon the reasonableness of the parties involved and their attitudes to it. This is always true to some extent about the operations of most clauses. However, it becomes less important when there is a clearly defined relationship such as current assets to current liabilities, compared with a clause such as we are now considering where there is a high level of interpretation and subjectivity. It is therefore important that you feel confident with your institutional partner and I would suggest that one that is going to take little interest in the operations of your company is not going to be capable of readily appreciating the arguments you may wish to put forward to make a change in policy. You should feel confident about being given an objective hearing and although this is not a guarantee that you will necessarily achieve success, it does make the problem one which it is in your power to control and success will be dependent upon the strength of your arguments and no other reasons.

5 Voting control

Unless there is more than one institution involved it is unlikely that the bank will have more than 50 per cent of the voting shares in the company. Obviously if the institutions have more than 50 per cent they have voting control of the company and they have no need to have clauses in a shareholders agreement to provide them with that capability. The purpose of obtaining voting control is generally very closely specified and it is not normally intended that it should be a device whereby the bank ends up running the company. One of the most common occurrences for inclusion of this clause is if there are preference shares with an agreed rate of dividend payable. Even though the preference shares may have a dividend due to them the directors can, if they wish, recommend that the dividend is not paid and if this course of action is supported at the annual general meeting by the shareholders then no dividend will be paid. To guard against this problem the bank will construct a mechanism whereby if the dividend on the preference shares is in arrears by more than a certain period, say six months, then the preference shares become enfranchised and have sufficient votes to call an annual general meeting and pass an extraordinary resolution to pay the dividend. When this action has been taken the preference shares cease to have their ability to vote and revert to their normal powers until the circumstances which trigger the voting rights occur again (in this case an overdue dividend payment).

From a practical viewpoint these types of controls should not present a problem if they are only enforcing what you have agreed to undertake anyway. It is important that the purpose is clearly defined and the resolution which they can carry. Otherwise they could have more far-reaching consequences. Therefore it is wise to spend some time understanding them.

6 Form of shareholding

This may or may not be referred to in the shareholders agreement. The actual definition of the various classes of shareholding will be undertaken in the Articles of Association. However, it may well be that certain rights which attach to these shares are mentioned in the shareholders agreement if they are considered to be conditions which the company does not wish to be generally known such as an agreed distribution policy even if there is no statutory right for the shares to receive a dividend in the Articles.

A clause is often inserted at this point to ensure that if the management team dispose of their shareholding then they are obliged to find a purchaser for the bank's shares at the same price. The rationale for this is that the bank back the management team and if they decide to leave the business the bank would like the opportunity to consider selling its shareholding as the circumstances for remaining with the company will have changed considerably.

7 Borrowing powers

It is normal for there to be borrowing powers of the directors defined in the Articles of Association but these are expressed in fairly wide terms, sometimes a multiple of net worth. There will normally be gearing restrictions in term loan agreements. Therefore these borrowing powers in the shareholders agreement are intended to be relevant only as long as the bank is a shareholder in the company and then only as a fallback position. It is obviously essential that the borrowing power limitations in the shareholders agreement allow the company to borrow its existing credit facilities and that it is not envisaged that there will be any breaches in the future. There should be substantial margins available for new borrowings should they become necessary as this clause should only be used to limit what could be regarded as a very extreme borrowing position. It is not being used to protect an exposed position such as it is with an unsecured loan covenant. In these circumstances, if more unsecured lenders are allowed to provide facilities to the company then in the case of a failure there is a lower payment to the lenders from the assets of the company. From a shareholder's viewpoint this is also true but it is of lesser significance because generally the payment expected by a shareholder in these circumstances is very low or zero and therefore a shareholder inserts this clause to prevent foolhardy behaviour rather than to protect a specific position.

8 Limitation of remuneration

This is always a contentious clause as it can seem to infringe upon the rights of the management team as owners. However, it can easily be envisaged that a bank can be in a very weak position as a minority shareholder in that the management team can vote themselves whatever salaries they wish even to the point of removing all profit from the company. This is clearly not a desirable situation as it can reduce the ability of the company to pay dividends. To prevent these circumstances occurring it is normal for there to be a clause limiting the remuneration that the management team can pay to themselves. There are several ways of structuring such an arrangement. The simplest from the bank's viewpoint is to have the power of veto over directors' remuneration. This is not always acceptable to the management and sometimes a figure is inserted into the agreement as an upper limit on remuneration and then this is increased each year by a factor such as the retail price index. It should be remembered that whatever is written in the shareholders agreement can be broken if all parties agree to it. However, what indexing achieves is that it allows a regular increase in the amount which can be paid out in directors' remuneration without having to refer back to all parties in the shareholders agreement. This can cause problems with the bank because it could allow the directors to increase their salaries even though the company might be making losses. Another approach is to link the remuneration to a percentage of profitability which prevents that particular set of circumstances arising.

Perhaps the most effective method is to set up a remuneration committee which comprises two people, normally the managing director and an independent non-executive director, quite often the chairman of the company, and this committee fix remuneration for the management team. The main advantage of this approach is that it does not rely upon any specific formula and is sufficiently flexible to take account of changes in circumstances when they arise without having to try to anticipate them when drafting the clause.

9 Pre-emption rights

These particular rights to the disposal of shareholdings are constructed to ensure that existing shareholders have a prior right to purchase any shares when they become available. This obviously can only apply to shareholdings that are unquoted because to have such a structure with quoted shares would make dealings too cumbersome and prevent transactions so that it would not be worthwhile trying to make a market in the shares. The way in which pre-emption rights normally operate is that a shareholder with a particular class of share wishes to sell his shares and finds someone who wishes to purchase them but before he can carry out the transaction he has to inform the company of his intentions. The company will then circulate shareholders with that class of share informing them of the amount and price that the shares will be dealt at. This is normally undertaken by the company secretary who invites the shareholders to submit indications of their interest at that price and in that amount. If there are several shareholders who wish to purchase the shares then they are normally allotted on a pro rata basis. If there is no interest by this class of shareholding the agreement may require that further existing classes of shareholders have to be circulated and confirmation obtained that they have no interest in purchasing the shares before they can be disposed of to an external shareholder.

This is to ensure that substantial changes in shareholdings cannot take place without the existing shareholders having an opportunity to purchase shares. It is normally required to any new shareholder that they enter into the existing shareholders agreement so that they are bound by whatever obligations the outgoing shareholder has entered into.

It can be seen that equity investment is a more complex operation than lending and that it requires more complex controls when undertaking it. Nevertheless, these controls are there for specific purposes and if you understand what their objectives are you are then in a position to assess whether they are likely to cause you any problems in the future. If they are going to, you can then set about seeking to slacken them so that their impact is reduced.

Chapter 5

AN EXAMPLE OF A FUNDING PACKAGE

When is equity investment appropriate?

The purpose of this chapter is to discuss a request for finance to illustrate the points covered in the preceding chapters. It will consider whether equity investment is appropriate in these particular circumstances and if so how it should be provided. Banks recognise that rightly or wrongly there is normally a reluctance on the part of existing shareholders in a business to consider equity as a method of financing in seeking to meet their requirements. Other forms of finance are normally preferred and tried first and, ignoring structural considerations, this approach is entirely logical.

As a holder of equity in a business, if that business can produce a return of 20 per cent pa on capital then if this rate of return can be achieved on new projects and funds can be borrowed for the new project at 16 per cent pa then that 4 per cent additional profit is completely available to shareholders. Whereas if the business is financed by equity, which results in the existing shareholders being diluted to, say, 75 per cent of their existing holding (ie an amount equal to one-third of the existing shareholders equity is issued to fund the project), then 15 per cent additional profit, ie 75 per cent of 20 per cent, would be available to the existing shareholders who in turn would only be entitled to 75 per cent of the existing profitability. Therefore, for this particular transaction to be attractive to them, additional profitability has to be greater than 25 per cent of the existing profitability for the existing shareholders to be better off. Whereas if it is financed by loans the existing shareholders are better off at any interest rate lower than 20 per cent pa, a much less stringent requirement.

Equity investment is therefore appropriate when the financial requirement of the business cannot be met by the existing shareholders or by conventional loan finance. Other things being equal, the availability of loan finance as viewed by the bank is a function of:

- the quantity and quality of earnings and cash flow relative to the size of the financing proposed
- the availability of security
- the availability of other support eg grants, incentives, guarantees such as can be provided by the government in certain circumstances

The amount which the bank feels unable to finance conventionally will be viewed as equity investment and there will be the same pressures upon potential equity investors as there are on existing shareholders to minimise the amount of equity and increase the amount of conventional loan finance to ensure that there is the maximum gearing effect upon equity earnings as discussed above.

The following example highlights the numerical analysis behind the proposal and its risk reward structure for a development capital transaction which includes conventional financing as well.

Summary of the transaction

Amount:	£500,000
Purpose:	To enable the company to produce and market a fully developed new product
FINANCED AS FOLLOWS	
Secured loan:	£300,000
Equity:	£200,000
	£500,000
SECURITY	The loan is secured by a mortgage debenture which is a fixed charge over certain assets such as property and a floating charge over all the assets.
	The repayment terms are a five year loan with a two year period at the beginning when no repayments are to be made (known as a holiday) and

then three equal annual repayments of £100,000 over the final three years.

PROFIT & LOSS:

	Before investment	*After investment*
Profit before tax and interest	£200,000	£200,000
Interest (rate assumed 15%)	(Nil)	(£45,000)
	£200,000	£155,000
Taxation at 25%	(50,000)	(38,750)
Earnings	£150,000	£116,250

BALANCE SHEET:

Working capital	£150,000	£500,000
Fixed assets	£100,000	£250,000
	£250,000	£750,000
Net worth	£250,000	£450,000
	Nil	£300,000
	£250,000	£750,000

It can be seen that of the £500,000 injected into the company £150,000 is used for the purchase of new fixed assets and £350,000 of the funding is used for working capital.

Projections

The company presents a package to the bank which shows that the summarised profit and loss balance sheet and cash flows for the existing business maintain profitability in the short term and in the longer term generate sufficient cash flows and earnings to repay the loan and pay dividends on the equity. However, for the first two years the cash flow will not be substantial until the project becomes established.

Value of assets for security purposes (after investigation by the bank)

Fixed assets	£100,000
Working capital	£260,000
	£360,000

Approach taken by banks in developing the structure

The company has come along and asked the bank for £500,000 to develop a new product which has been proven and market tested. The situation is over-simplified to enable the major points of structure to be discussed but there is an implicit assumption that the bank has examined the proposal and wants to try to undertake the transaction. This means that it has satisfied itself with areas such as the capability of the management team to control their existing business and accommodate the new project, the market assumptions for the new product and the production facilities required to manufacture it. Given that these aspects have been covered the question which now needs to be considered is what reason the bank had for providing £300,000 of the total funds by way of loan and £200,000 by way of equity.

The easiest way of approaching this first of all is by regarding the equity as a residual requirement and ignoring whether it presents an attractive equity return to an investor. Instead we shall just consider what the maximum amount of funding is that the bank would consider making available as a loan.

Loan finance

By way of an example let us consider what would be the case if £500,000 was borrowed to finance the transaction and what would be the effects upon the company's balance sheet.

Earnings

As far as the earnings stream is concerned we are told that the existing level of earnings, ie £200,000, is maintainable while developing the new project, which implies that resources will not be diverted from this area and future earnings from this source jeopardised. We therefore have a maintainable earnings stream of £200,000 pa. If £500,000 is borrowed at, say, an interest rate of 15 per cent pa this will have an interest cost of £75,000. With £200,000 of profit before interest and tax this will result in interest being covered 2.6x. This is not an outrageously low interest cover but it is beginning to look rather thin. As a rule of thumb a minimum of 3x interest cover is often looked upon as an acceptable level in a small company.

If we assume this interest charge then the cash flow available to repay the loan would be:

Profit before interest and tax	£200,000
Interest	£75,000
Pre-tax profits	£125,000
Tax at 25 per cent	£31,250
	£93,750

Free cash flow is £93,750 and this is assuming that there are no other demands upon the cash flow whereas we are told that the projections do not allow any repayment at all in the first two years. It is likely therefore that it will take around seven to ten years to repay this facility on the basis of existing earnings. This is quite a long time for a company of this size to be borrowing for and such that taken into consideration with the thin interest cover this would not be regarded as an acceptable set of circumstances. The quality of earnings in a company of this size, ie the degree to which you can rely upon there being consistent earnings year after year, is very low simply because a company with the size of profitability such as this one can very easily be moved into loss and therefore an unsecured facility for a long term would not be acceptable to a bank.

Security

We have looked at the earnings streams as a source of repayment and we now need to consider the opportunities available for repayment if the earnings stream should fail. This second source of repayment is security and as the assets of the business are not used to support any existing borrowings we need to consider what value we can look to these for and how. By taking fixed charges and floating charges over the company's assets and looking to them as providing a value, albeit in a forced sale situation, we can anticipate what sort of value we might receive. We are in fact told that the figure for this company is around £360,000. Because of the uncertainty over a loan which will take up to ten years to repay the bank is going to look for full cover from any security and probably a small margin to allow for any mistaken assumptions when placing value upon the assets. With a forced sale value on the assets of £360,000 this does not allow full cover for the loan and would provide a poor argument for a ten year loan of £500,000.

Balance sheet

We also need to consider the presentation of the balance sheet to the outside world if £500,000 were borrowed by a company with a net worth of £250,000. This would result in a gearing level of 200 per cent (ie shareholders' funds £250,000: borrowings £500,000). In these circumstances trade creditors may well feel a little uneasy about extending credit and that could cause a need for further borrowing facilities as trade credit is withdrawn.

It would therefore seem by considering the three criteria above that £500,000 as a loan would not be a particularly attractive proposition for the bank to lend as both the earnings stream and security are weak for this amount.

Determining the amount of the loan facility

We now know what is unacceptable from the bank's viewpoint. What we need to work towards is identifying a level at which the bank would be comfortable to provide facilities. It can be seen that because we are dealing with the inter-relationships of at least three elements — earnings, security and balance sheet — there is no particular point which is precisely right. Different individuals will feel comfortable at different levels because they will each have a different way of interpreting the facts and feel capable of attributing higher levels of confidence to different aspects. However, overall there should be a general consensus band which at least 90 per cent of the institutions would feel represented a logical level of exposure and one which could be justified in reasonable argument to a credit committee.

To arrive at this acceptable level we have to repeat the process which was described above with lower levels of borrowings and compensating increases in the equity of the business so that a total of £500,000 is still invested in the company, part by way of equity and part by way of loan. This can be arrived at by way of an iterative process undertaking many calculations of the situation at different levels of borrowings. In practice it is possible to shortcut this approach by identifying the limiting factor at an early stage and using that variable alone to determine the borrowing level.

In the example above the most critical area would seem to be either the security or the balance sheet constraints and therefore one of these must be selected to determine an acceptable borrowing level. The area of the balance sheet is less easy to be specific about than security. Therefore it is probably easiest to select security and work through an example determined only by the security level. As we identified earlier, for a company of this size and a term facility, the quality of earnings, ie the dependability of a maintainable level of profitability, is fairly low and therefore greater dependence has to be placed on the value of the security. Being reasonably prudent and allowing for a 20 per cent margin on the security the forced sale valuation on the assets of £360,000 would support a borrowing level of £300,000. Having identified this level it now needs to be checked in terms of the other constraints. From an earnings consideration a borrowing level of £300,000 would incur an interest charge of £45,000 pa assuming an interest rate of 15 per cent pa. Profit before interest and tax of £200,000 would provide an interest cover of

$$\frac{£200,000}{£45,000}$$

which is 4.4x covered. This is a perfectly acceptable level of interest cover and given that it is not envisaged that profitability will fluctuate violently then it should not cause a bank to feel concerned. The impact of this level of borrowings upon the balance sheet now has to be examined. If £300,000 is to be made available in the form of a loan facility then it follows from our earlier arguments that £500,000–£300,000, ie £200,000, will be made available by way of equity investment. If this is so then shareholders' funds will increase by £200,000 from £250,000 to £450,000 and borrowings will be £300,000. These circumstances then would result in a gearing level of £300,000 to £450,000, ie 67 per cent. This is obviously substantially better than the previous 200 per cent and would not be regarded as unacceptable for a company of this size with a secured facility. It indicates to outside observers such as trade creditors that the company is not borrowing more money from the banks than its shareholders' funds and therefore the shareholders are still the major stakeholders in the business in terms of money employed. As a broad indication, were the company to go into liquidation the assets that were represented by shareholders' funds would be available to meet the bank's debts and to the extent that there was a surplus then this would be available to meet other creditors' requirements over and above whatever was realised by the assets appropriate to their respective debts. This may be a fairly broad brush approach but it serves to act as a general indicator of the financial stability of the business.

The final point is that because the company is borrowing only 60 per cent of the total amount it can repay it comfortably over a shorter period, eg five years. This in turn enables the bank to feel a little more relaxed about the facility. As was mentioned earlier the solution arrived at is not unique. It is possible that because of the strength of the new project a bank might say that it is prepared to lend £350,000 and it will be difficult to argue that this was not an appropriate view to take without going into the assumptions for the projections. However, it is unlikely that generally a company would be able to raise amounts significantly outside of that range for a similar type of facility.

All this serves to indicate how important it is to make sure that your proposition is presented in the most favourable light to an institution because it can make a considerable difference to the equity participation that is sought and this would be purely from interpretation and 'feel' of the company. It is really the bank shading its views to the top or bottom end of the generally acceptable exposure band.

Equity finance

Up to now we have treated the equity as a residual when trying to determine the maximum amount of loan financing that could be obtained from the bank. This is fine from the lender's viewpoint because initially at least all he is concerned about is that equity capital is provided if loan finance is to be made available. This is because the requirements and entitlements of equity investment rank after those of lenders and therefore any form of equity will support and bolster the position of a lender, particularly a secured lender who will receive the benefit of all the equity investment that is not used to reduce permanently the other debts of the company which do not rank ahead of the lender.

However, as we have mentioned previously, the equity investor will have his own requirements to meet before he makes any form of investment and the approach of treating equity investment as a residual does not attempt to apply any form of evaluation of the risk/reward criteria. To do this he will concentrate upon the prospects of the business (upside) and the converse which is the event of failure (downside). This is in itself a difficult enough proposition but he must also try to place his own estimates of probability on the likelihood of each event occurring and then try to ascertain whether he is receiving an adequate reward. This again, like the loan, results in a high degree of subjectivity which can easily work against a badly prepared or poorly presented case.

In arriving at the amount of the investment the financial institution in this case needs to decide what it would require as a stake in the business if it were to subscribe £200,000 worth of equity. This requires that a valuation is placed upon the business and to do this whichever approach is used there needs to be an assessment of the value of the cash flow.

Traditionally there are three ways in which equity valuation is measured, namely:

(1) Earnings stream

(2) Asset value

(3) Synergy

These are different approaches but they are all placing a monetary value at a point in time upon the flow of cash to be received some time in the future.

(1) Earnings stream This is the cash to be received from the business and will include anticipated dividends together with proceeds from an anticipated sale sometime in the future.

(2) Asset value The cash flow here is the money to be received from a liquidation of the business and the proceeds from that which are distributed to the shareholders.

(3) Synergy This flow of income results from merging the business with another company which should then result in savings in overheads by the two businesses and possibly a realisation of any assets surplus to requirements.

As a general rule investment institutions are only concerned with the first method of valuation because their circumstances do not allow them to take an independent course of action that could bring about the necessary events that would make the methods of valuation in (2) and (3) relevant. This is because they normally do not have a controlling interest which would enable them to realise assets and similarly they do not have existing businesses that would produce benefits of synergy. However, this does not mean to say that they will not back management teams who make proposals that involve the sort of events that give rise to cash flows mentioned in (2) and (3). In these circumstances the method of evaluation would take into consideration the cash flows which were generated from the realisation of assets and/or synergy. The investment bank will normally therefore consider the earnings streams that will be generated by the company as a continuing business both from dividends and from an anticipated sale of the shares. This is transformed into valuing the company on a multiple of its post tax earnings (price/earnings ratio), the argument being that the post tax earnings have two elements, that which is distributed by the company (the dividend) and that which is retained in the company to be used to generate future earnings and hopefully higher dividend streams. The business is then valued on a suitable multiple of post tax profits which is obtained by seeking quoted companies in similar businesses and then applying a discount to the price/earnings ratio that these companies are valued at to allow for the fact that this business is unquoted and probably smaller and therefore more vulnerable. The discount is normally around 20/30 per cent. Traditionally earnings are calculated on a normalised tax charge, ie the level of taxation that a company would expect to incur. If this is not to be applied there has to be a reason why the business will incur tax charges at a different rate on a continuing basis, not just for a year or two.

In the example we are considering £200,000 is being subscribed for 30 per cent of the enlarged equity, ie valuing the company at:

$$£200{,}000 \times \frac{1}{0.3} = £660{,}000$$

This would mean that the price/earnings ratio was:

$$\frac{£660{,}000}{£116{,}250} = 5.7x$$

This price/earnings ratio was calculated by reference to quoted companies in similar businesses and then discounted; presumably they were on P/Es of between 7x and 8x. If it had been, say, 6, then a P/E of 4 may be appropriate in which case on earnings of £116,250 this would value the business at around £465,000. Then on the basis of an investment of £200,000 this would require a holding in the company of 45 per cent which might be too high for some institutions to hold on their own. They might well want to share it with someone.

The price/earnings method of valuation by comparison with quoted companies requires that it is possible to identify companies that are directly comparable with the target business both in terms of activity and record because a company's price/earnings ratio is the result of a complex relationship between many determinants including the history of the company and its capability to maintain profits or otherwise. It is normal to use the earnings in the price/earnings calculation either as latest achieved profit or anticipated profitability no longer than 12 months away. These are referred to as historic and prospective price/earnings ratios respectively and a lower multiple is placed on forecast profitability than achieved profitability. Similarly, the company should not be valued on an exceptional year because the concept of a price/earnings figure is a purchase of so many years' earnings and it will only be appropriate to use a particular year if it was considered that the level of profitability was maintainable. Clearly, if a year is exceptional then by definition those earnings are not maintainable.

The institution will also use a discounted cash flow calculation based upon certain assumptions to determine what sort of reward it could realistically expect from investment of this nature. A simplistic approach might be £200,000 invested in year one for 30 per cent of the equity and it will generate, say, gross dividends of, say, 10 per cent pa and profitability will grow to £400,000 pre-tax over the next five years at which point the company will anticipate seeking a flotation. If an assumption is made that a company of this type would achieve a flotation P/E of 10, on a conservative basis, then this would value the whole business at £4,000,000. Thirty per cent of £4m is £1.2m, a compound growth rate of approximately 38 per cent pa to which must be added the dividend yield of 10 per cent pa making a total return of 48 per cent pa. This figure by itself does not mean very much. What the institution has to assess is what sort of risk attaches to the transaction, eg whether the proposition is a venture capital deal or a development capital deal. In the example we are considering it would seem to be a development capital deal in terms of the stability of the existing business and the magnitude of the new funding requirements, in which case 48 per cent pa would seem to be an acceptable potential return.

When making a presentation to a bank it is often better merely to indicate the funding requirements and not seek to stipulate the amount of equity you would anticipate that it should attract. This is a highly emotive area and at the end of the day it is a result of negotiation. However, to be able to negotiate effectively you should understand how the institution will view its position and seek to ask it to justify any figures it puts forward.

Chapter 6

FURTHER CONSIDERATIONS WHEN SEEKING FUNDING

Reducing the Equity Risk

So far we have been considering a proposal which is self-contained from the institutional viewpoint. That is to say the institution considers the proposal by looking at the strength of the covenant of the applicant and then decides whether it should be regarded as lending or equity risk. It is possible that a particular transaction could appear as an equity risk because, from the institutional viewpoint, there is a shortfall in the nature of the security. A classic occurrence of this is a property development transaction and an example of how this might occur is shown below:

- Assume that Company A wishes to borrow the full amount of £600,000 to develop a property and then dispose of it.
- Institution X will only lend 75% of development costs.

When A approaches X for 100% financing of the project, ie £600,000, then X will assess its risk and on the basis that the proposal is sensible and that A can show a record of having successfully carried out these transactions before, X may well say that it will lend up to £450,000 to develop the project. In these circumstances X is looking for a contribution of £150,000 from A that will not rank ahead of X.

This can be regarded as a normal form of banking prudence, ie never lend 100% of the project because the developer has no incentive to continue if things go wrong. There are many arguments for and against this approach and I do not wish to confuse the point by discussing them in this example; suffice to say that at any time it is nearly always possible to find institutions who will support each viewpoint.

If now X will only make available up to £450,000 on the basis of this application it may well be possible that this position can be changed, if A revises its approach to X and puts forward the proposal that additional security can be offered to cover the shortfall of £150,000. It could well be that A has another property which has no charges or mortgages upon it and can be valued at £200,000. This can be offered to X and the security calculation will be as follows:

Original Property valued @	£600,000 x 75% =	£450,000
New Property valued @	£200,000 x 75% =	£150,000
	£800,000	£600,000

X can now justify lending A £600,000; however this does, of course, assume that all other things are equal and that the cashflow from the project is adequate to service the facility. In this case a transaction which was originally viewed as having £150,000 of equity risk attached to it has been transformed into a lending risk by enhancing the proposal through the addition of further security from outside the project.

Forms of security that may be requested

From the previous section it can be seen that by offering an enhanced form of recourse to the institution it may be possible in certain circumstances to meet the credit criteria for a facility at a higher level. It is probably sensible at this point to consider how an institution views security because this will have a direct bearing on what value it will place upon different assets that you may be considering suggesting for this purpose.

As we have already mentioned in Chapter 5, security is taken by an institution as a secondary source of repayment when the primary source fails. This means that the institution has already evaluated the cashflow coming from the primary source, ie the project, and satisfied itself that it is reasonable to assume that all these events are likely to occur as proposed. Security is then taken as an insurance policy in case some unforeseen event occurs which disrupts the primary source of cash and makes it inadequate for one reason or another; the institution will still have the security to turn to and achieve repayment. It should ideally represent an independent source of repayment but this may not always be perfectly achievable.

It should be noted that banks generally take the view that they do not lend solely against security; they sometimes refer to this rather derogatorily as 'pawnbroking'. A pawnbroker will pay no attention at all to the ability of the client borrowing the money to repay the debt. It is almost regarded as a bonus if the debt is repaid and the pledge redeemed; instead the pawnbroker concentrates solely on the value of the security as his only certain source of repayment. A consequence of this is that the pawnbroker's pledge is a very good example of what constitutes acceptable security. It is also worth remarking at this juncture that it is extremely rare for a pawnbroker to experience a bad debt through failure of security, which serves to underline my point.

Let us now consider what criteria an institution would apply to the taking of security:

(a) Title

In the event that it becomes necessary to rely upon the security then the institution needs to know that it has title to the security. The reason for this is that to realise the value of the security it would normally be necessary to dispose of the security and that would entail passing title to a third party. If there were any impediment to prevent the institution doing this, then it needs to be recognised at the outset when the institution is assessing the value of the security. For example, if the institution were offered a second charge over a property behind a first charge limited to say £50,000, then the value of the security would be reduced by £50,000. This is because the holder of the second charge could not force a sale of the property against the will of the first charge-holder, without paying off the first charge-holder and thereby becoming the holder of the first charge.

(b) Value

It would seem obvious that the value of a security should be easily ascertainable and stable over time because the purpose of taking security is to ensure that should it be required, the value can be obtained at or above the level at which it was originally anticipated. However, by reflecting upon the nature of the values of assets for a short time, it can easily be seen that this is a difficult, if not impossible, objective to achieve. Prices tend to move over time and the more volatile the value of a security, the more uncertain is the estimate of its value in the future. Therefore, the institution holding the security will apply a discount to any value estimated, to allow for this level of volatility or uncertainty and still have a base value which can be applied in a lending proposal. In the example shown above it was suggested that a 25% discount would be applied when valuing property. If the security had been an insurance policy or government stocks then a much lower level of discount would be possible, perhaps only 10% may have been considered appropriate. As a general rule the more specialised the asset the fewer potential purchasers and the larger the discount applied when assessing the value for security purposes.

(c) Ease of realisation

The simpler it is to dispose of an asset for money then, normally, the less expensive are the costs associated with the realisation. A security can be down-valued if it takes time and money to achieve a sale. For example, once possession has been obtained, it is fairly easy to sell a car and there are many potential purchasers together with trade guides indicating value depending upon condition and mileage; within two or three days a sale should be made. Compare this to selling a property such as a private hospital, where advertising is necessary and transaction costs are quite substantial. For an institution, if time is required to achieve a realisation, then interest costs are accruing during the period until the money is received, increasing the exposure of the institution at the very time when it wants its exposure reducing.

As we mentioned earlier pawnbroking security addresses these three points in a most satisfactory way. A pledge, say a gold ring, is handed over the counter for a loan and the loan is made upon a value of around 70% of the scrap value of the gold. No account is taken of the intrinsic workmanship of the jewellery. The ring is pledged and placed in a safe on the pawnbroker's premises. If the loan is not repaid then all the pawnbroker has to do is walk to the safe, take out the ring and sell it either in the window of his shop, at auction or as scrap gold. The question of title is dealt with because he is given title to the ring through the pledge document. He has tested the gold himself and knows the value of scrap gold, which he has discounted severely before making the loan. He has little problem with realisation because he has possession of the article and there are many purchasers of scrap gold, which is the very worst assessment of the value.

(d) Direct and collateral security

Institutions frequently refer to security by dividing it into two broad classes. The first is that referred to as a direct security and can be regarded as the security provided by the applicant for funding, namely the borrower. This can be a charge or call upon the assets of the borrower and is exactly the same whether we are talking about a personal or a corporate borrower. The second is described as collateral security and this is security which is provided by third parties to the transaction to support the obligations of the borrower. An example of this is when a director of a company provides security to support the company's borrowings. An easier way of looking at this is to consider direct security as coming from inside the deal and collateral security as coming from outside the deal.

(e) Types of security

How institutions choose to take security will vary and depend largely upon two factors. The first and normally most important is the nature of the transaction being funded and the second is what is available from other sources; remember the bank cannot have what you have not got. Under the headings listed below I have sought to define types of security by employing descriptions which are practically helpful when considering security as a potential borrower.

(i) **Mortgage** Here title to the assets, be they property, stocks and shares, life policies etc are transferred to the lender so that in the event that the debt is not repaid as originally agreed, sale of the assets can be achieved.

(ii) **Lien** This is the right of the bank to retain property handled by the bank in the ordinary course of business, until the debt is repaid. With a banker's lien there is also the power of sale in certain circumstances; therefore, if you undertake all your banking with one institution bear this in mind.

(iii) **Pledge** In this case the bank has negotiable securities deposited with it, ie possession gives title. It does not have to be the goods themselves, as when negotiating a letter of credit; bills of lading give title to the goods which are physically deposited in a warehouse somewhere and held to the bank's order. The bank would normally have the power to retain the goods and sell them to recover the debt.

(iv) **Hypothecation** This is a charge over goods which are not in the bank's possession; the owner undertakes to give the bank possession when called upon to do so.

(v) **Guarantee and indemnity** I have included these two forms together because normally what is referred to as a bank's standard form of guarantee is in fact an indemnity. A guarantee is security given by a third party to a lender to meet the obligations of a borrower in the event that a borrower fails to perform his obligations. Before a guarantee can be called upon it is necessary to make demand upon the borrower. An indemnity is a similar obligation except that the lender does not have to make demand upon the borrower. Recourse can be sought directly from the indemnifier.

(f) Guarantees

A guarantee is one of the most frequently requested forms of additional security, particularly from directors of smaller companies who approach institutions for facilities. The argument commonly put forward to justify this is that the provision of a guarantee by directors is evidence that the directors believe in their proposals and gives the institution confidence that they will not attempt to walk away from the project. This may or may not be appropriate and each case has to be looked at on its own merits. However there is no doubt that care needs to be exercised when considering giving a guarantee. The following statements have been made cynically or otherwise about giving guarantees:

- He that is surety for a stranger shall smart for it and he that hateth suretyship is sure: Proverbs 11:15.
- The definition of a guarantee is a fool with a pen in his hand.
- A guarantee might be defined as where one man who cannot pay gets another man who cannot pay to say that he will.

There is general concern about guarantees and rightly so, because a guarantee is easy to take and when it is taken it is never given with the intention that it will ever need to be called upon. Consequently calling upon a guarantee normally entails a degree of resentment by the guarantor, together with annoyance. I have been guilty of giving guarantees and having them called upon me so I am aware that often it is impossible to get a transaction financed unless a guarantee is given; I would simply make the following observations:

(i) Ensure that you believe in the transaction you are guaranteeing.

(ii) Ensure that you understand the transaction you are guaranteeing.

(iii) Ensure that you explain to the bank that you are prepared to give a guarantee but you want it limited to an amount that you are good for and not some multiple of many times your net worth.

(g) Supported guarantees

When taking a guarantee an institution may well look to see that there is some tangible value behind the guarantee which can be realised in the event that a call is made upon the guarantee. The form of support taken can vary, but it is quite commonly represented by a charge upon the home of the guarantor, usually because this is often the largest tangible asset that most people own. Here too it is impossible to give any specific advice about undertaking such a course of action because again it may well be the only course available to obtaining finance and only you can assess whether the risks are worth taking. It is however something which should not be entered into lightly as the consequences can be severe because perhaps, not only do you lose your business, but you place your home at risk if things do not work out as expected.

(h) Foreign currency loans

Over the last few years there has been more awareness by the general public about the possibility of borrowing in a currency other than that which is regarded as domestic ie companies which are sterling based could borrow in eurocurrencies. This has even spread to the UK domestic mortgage market where it is quite possible to see advertisements in many papers encouraging people to borrow long term in currency other than sterling. How then should a business approach such facilities and what are the risks which attach to these products ?

The first points which should be considered are:

(i) What is going to be purchased with the funds and in what currency?

(ii) Where will the repayment come from and in what currency?

If we take the following example:

- Company A is a UK-based manufacturing company.
- It wishes to borrow £500,000 to purchase a factory in the UK.
- All company A's sales are in sterling.
- The period of the loan is ten years.

Because the UK has had relatively high levels of inflation in recent times and the government has been following policies of controlling inflation through the mechanism of high interest rates, then for the last few years UK interest rates compared to many European countries and the United States have been relatively higher at certain times. This has presented an opportunity for some rather unscrupulous providers of finance to suggest that a benefit could be achieved by borrowing in another currency where interest rates were relatively lower when compared with sterling. On the face of it this would appear a reasonable proposition and would most certainly be true if relationships between currencies and interest rates were static. However this is not so, because we live in a changing world and they are obviously dynamic and also because it is a fact that loans are generally required for a reasonably long period of time. These two basic conditions serve to increase the uncertainty in the transaction.

In the example, let us assume A borrows £500,000 from a bank, purchases the UK factory for £500,000 and then proceeds to repay the loan over ten years, having made annual interest payments of, say, approximately 10% pa, ie £50,000. A achieves his interest payments by using his sterling sales proceeds and also over the period of ten years accumulates sufficient sterling to make the capital repayment at the end.

Suppose that A were to borrow US dollars to purchase the factory: then, because the factory was being sold for a sterling price, A would have to calculate how many dollars would be needed to purchase £500,000 worth of sterling from his bank to give to the current owner of the factory. Let us assume that the sterling - US dollar exchange rate is £1 = $2. A would have to borrow $1,000,000 at the outset to purchase sufficient sterling to buy the factory. A would then have an obligation to pay interest on the $1,000,000 which was, say, at 7% because he would need a favourable sterling-dollar interest differential to induce him to borrow in dollars. A then has to find sufficient sterling from sales revenues to purchase dollars each year to make the interest payments and at the end of ten years make the capital repayment. If during the ten-year period the sterling-dollar rate stays at £1 = $2 then A is better off than if he had borrowed in sterling because of the cheaper interest rate differential, though all these purchases of dollars with sterling attract a commission for the institution carrying them out and therefore A would be worse off by the extent of his transaction charges.

If however the sterling-dollar rate moved against A, eg perhaps it finished at £1 = $1.5, then A would have to pay more sterling to achieve the same amount of dollars; for example, after ten years he would still owe $1,000,000 but he would need to pay £666,666 sterling to purchase them and make the repayment. This would only be worthwhile to A if the increase in the sterling value of the loan was offset by the sum of the sterling values of benefits obtained from the difference in the interest rate costs of borrowing in dollars rather than sterling. These benefits would need to be considered over the whole of the ten-year period and I have assumed, to make matters easier, that the interest rate differential can be fixed throughout the period by comparing the ten-year fixed rate in dollars with the ten-year fixed rate in sterling fixed at the time the loan is taken out. However this calculation works out, whether a profit or a loss is experienced, this is achieved by the borrower gambling that sterling-dollar exchange rate movements will move in a favourable manner over a ten-year period. Therefore, the borrower should be aware of these risks and consider whether they should be taken or not at the outset, not discover them halfway through the loan period. Historically there are examples of this type of open position going extremely wrong. During the 1970s there were occasions when UK companies were attracted to borrowing long term in Swiss francs because the Swiss franc rate was only 4% when in the United Kingdom rates were considerably higher. The problem was that the sterling-Swiss franc exchange rate moved steadily against a UK borrower in Swiss francs to the extent that some of the loans ended up being double the sterling amount that was originally borrowed.

This placed substantial and in some cases terminal pressure upon the borrower.

It is only by careful analysis of the risks that are inherent in borrowing in another currency, that a borrower can consider whether these can be minimised to a level where they become acceptable. The one change that would completely remove the risks that we have been foreseeing, ie those relating to exposures arising from having obligations in one currency and income in another, is if there was not a mismatch in currencies. If, for example, company A did not have all its sales in sterling but instead only part were domestic and some of the sales, the remainder, were made in the United States, then it would be possible for A to be paid dollars for their sales and as long as there were sufficient dollars to meet the loan obligations, there would be no need for A to use sterling to purchase dollars and thereby create an exchange risk. This does, of course, assume that A is confident that sales to the United States will continue for ten years to generate sufficient dollars to meet both interest and capital repayments.

There are other instruments which can be used to remove totally or in part the risks arising from exposure to foreign exchange. The most common of these is a forward exchange contract. There are other variations but essentially they all seek to protect a capital sum in one currency in terms of a fixed amount in another currency at some point in the future. It is unusual to get forward contracts for periods of ten years; they are more common for up to 12 - 24 months and they can easily be purchased from commercial banks. They are a mechanism which allows a future payment in one currency to be fixed in terms of a second currency as shown in the following example:

Company A expects to receive a payment of, say, $100,000 in 12 months' time as a result of a fixed price contract it has just signed with a company in the United States. To carry out this contract A has to purchase £30,000 worth of goods and services to manufacture the products to be sold. If A has worked out its pricing on the basis of a sterling - dollar rate of £1 = $2 then it would anticipate the following profit:

£1 = $2

Sales:	$100,000 @ £1 = $2 =	£50,000
Costs:	fixed in sterling =	£30,000
Profit:		£20,000

However the sterling - dollar rate is quite volatile (let us assume that at the end of the 12-month period it is £1 = $2.5); then the same contract produces a new level of profitability:

£1 = $2.5

Sales:	\$100,000 @ £1 = \$2.5 =	£40,000
Costs:	fixed in sterling =	£30,000
Profit:		£10,000

As can be seen the profit is halved through no other cause than the volatility of the exchange rates. Company A could take out a forward contract to sell its future receipt of \$100,000 for sterling in 12 months' time and the bank would quote a price in the forward contract at which the transaction would take place, eg £1 = \$2.1. This now means that the \$100,000 has been sold for £(100,000 ÷ 2.1) = £47,619. The contract means that A is now certain to receive a fixed amount of sterling instead of dollars at the end of 12 months which removes the exchange rate exposure from the contract and hence a large amount of uncertainty. You will notice that this has not been achieved without a cost but this reduction in profit is the price of removing the risk.

If we now look again at the example where A was borrowing \$1,000,000 to purchase a factory for £500,000; it could be possible for A to take out a forward contract for 12 months to cover his exchange risks on the first interest payment and the capital amount of the loan, so that if the sterling-dollar rate moved against him he was no worse off except for the costs attaching to covering the risk by purchasing the contract. If for example we consider A's obligations:

A has borrowed \$1,000,000 for ten years at 7% pa, then converted it to sterling at £1 = \$2, and used the £500,000 to purchase a factory. Over the first 12 months A has to make a payment of \$70,000 and he may wish to fix this amount in sterling now so that he knows exactly what he has to pay. Suppose he purchased a contract to purchase dollars in 12 months' time at £1 = \$1.9, then he knows he will have to pay £36,800, which is slightly more than the £35,000 he may have assumed at the current rate of £1 = \$2. A has removed the risk of making a loss on his first interest payment by fixing the sterling amount at the outset, because £36,800 is still less than the £50,000 he would have expected to pay in sterling at 10% pa and £1 = \$2. However, by so doing he has also removed the opportunity of taking advantage of the rates mainly in his favour and reducing his sterling cost; eg if the sterling dollar rate was £1 = \$2.1 in 12 months' time then A would only have to pay £33,000 for his \$70,000, a favourable improvement of £2,000.

The point of A covering his risk at the outset is to allow him to assess if he wishes to undertake the transaction now that the risks can be viewed in sterling.

FX Relationships

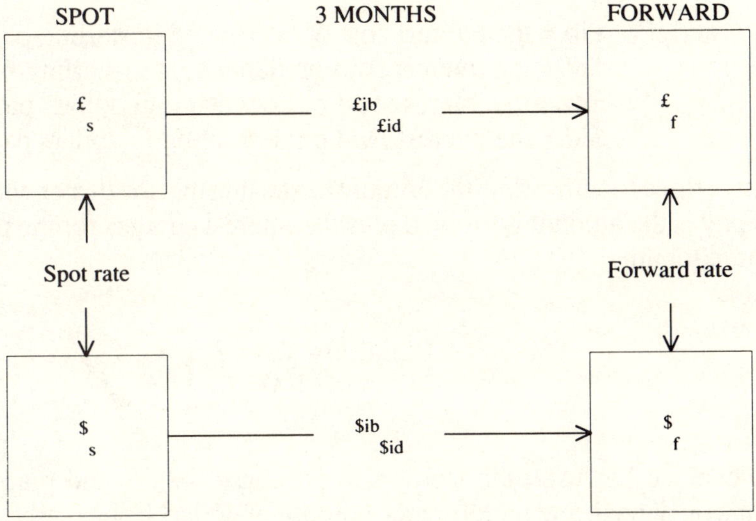

A cannot obtain forward cover for ten years but it may be possible for him to arrange a foreign currency loan whereby the principal can be switched into sterling at some time in the future at his request, probably with a suitable notice period, say three months. This allows A to have the opportunity to close out his foreign exchange position during the life of the loan at fairly minimal transaction costs. What this means in practice is that A may have been able to cover interest payments and the capital amount of the loan forward for, say, 12 months at costs which showed him a profit when compared with borrowing in sterling. However, at the end of 12 months he then seeks quotations to cover his interest and capital repayments but finds that the cost of these exceed the benefit of the interest differential between sterling and dollars; in other words he would be better off borrowing in sterling. If A has the option to switch his dollar loan back into sterling in three months' time he can make arrangements to do this and if necessary cover it with forward contracts to hedge his position and thereby limit the risk of the position deteriorating.

At this point it is worthwhile considering how theoretically forward foreign exchange contracts are calculated, because it is often suggested that forward exchange contracts can profitably provide cover on interest differential transactions. The relationships are shown in the diagram above. A foreign exchange dealer undertakes to write a contract to sell dollars in three months' time for sterling: what rate should he quote? The dealer will work out what it will cost him to borrow sterling now, buy the dollars in the spot market and then hold it for three months to sell for sterling which he will use to repay his borrowings in sterling.

If we suppose that the dealer borrows £50,000 and converts it at the spot rate of £1 = \$2 for \$100,000:

and if: £ib = the interest cost of borrowing in sterling pa
£id = the interest paid on depositing in sterling pa
\$ib = the interest cost of borrowing in dollars pa
\$id = the interest paid on depositing in dollars pa

Then in three months' time the amount of sterling that the dealer will have to repay is the amount borrowed plus the interest charges for the period, ie three months.
This is:

$$\pounds 50{,}000 + \left\{ 50{,}000 \times \frac{\pounds ib}{100} \times \frac{3}{12} \right\} = \pounds_f$$

However he has used the sterling to purchase dollars and placed the dollars on deposit and therefore the amount of dollars he has at the end of three months is:

$$\$100{,}000 + \left\{ \$100{,}000 \times \frac{\$id}{100} \times \frac{3}{12} \right\} = \$_f$$

Then the three-month forward rate that the dealer would quote would be calculated by £f/\$f. It can also be appreciated that the dealer is in a market where he is quoting two-way prices ie he is buying or selling dollars or buying or selling sterling; consequently if there were an inequality in one route then the market would operate to remove this fairly quickly. By this I mean that were it possible to make a profit by borrowing sterling, converting it to dollars and then holding it for three months, but taking out a foreign exchange contract it would allow you to make a profit by selling the dollars for sterling at a better rate than shown above; very quickly, if this particular dealer who was writing these contracts continued to do this, he would go broke because the whole marketplace would take advantage of this inequality. This is referred to as an arbitrage situation, ie where it is possible to buy in one market and sell in another at a profit. I have taken time to illustrate this point because if it is appreciated that if borrowing in a non-domestic currency was purely a transaction to take advantage of interest rate differentials and that apart from this there was no trading reason to be in the currency, then when it is understood how forward contracts are calculated, it should serve as a warning to examine very carefully the claims of any offers which undertake to maintain the benefits of an interest rate differential while providing a fully-covered exchange rate position.

Chapter 7

UNCONVENTIONAL SHORT-TERM TRANSACTIONS

The Main Attributes

We have considered the possibility of approaching institutions for long-term equity financing or shorter-term loan financing and, generally, we have assumed that the necessity to produce a detailed proposal has meant that the nature of the funding requirement was to be of a strategic nature and probably to be in place for some time. However, there are occasions for some companies when they have a need for funding requirement which is not long term, but it is disproportionately large when compared to the normal borrowing capabilities of the company. Such a transaction has been hinted at before in the previous chapter, when considering a property development transaction which was too large for the company on the basis of a conventional banking approach, but in certain circumstances could be changed by the provision of additional security to allow the bank to advance funds. This is not the only example which could be given but it is a good one to draw out the major attributes of cashflow, size, timing and expertise.

Cashflow

This is a fundamental requirement of all these types of transaction in that the cashflow from the project must always be adequate to repay capital and reward risk. In the example of property development (see chapter 6, p81) the only reason that the bank did not advance the loan initially was because of a security shortfall; there was adequate cashflow to allow a 100% loan to be made. Another way of describing these transactions is that they must have the capability of being self-liquidating, ie there are no external sources of cash required to effect repayment after the original financing. Trade transactions should all be self-liquidating otherwise the trader would be making a loss, ie he would be paying more for his goods than he would be selling them for.

Size

These transactions fall outside the conventional funding requirements because of their size relative to the company which is seeking to undertake them. It may well be that for a larger company the transaction being proposed would be regarded as a perfectly acceptable risk and would be financed by a normal loan facility with full recourse to the company.

Timing

When funding is being sought for a property transaction the bank considering proceeding with the development has to give some consideration to whether the development already has a potential purchaser or tenant or whether it is a purely speculative transaction in that the purchaser still has to be found. If the situation is the latter then the institution has to consider the risk that, even when the building is complete, it is possible that it may not be able to be sold for some considerable time. During this time there is interest accruing on the loan which was taken out to build the development; these interest costs increase the total costs of the development and consequently reduce the profitability of the scheme when eventually it is sold. There are occasions when the carrying costs are so great that they eventually erode all the profit margin in the development and even though the scheme may have been built to budget, it cannot be sold to budget and a loss arises.

Expertise

This is a significant requirement without which it is unlikely that an institution would proceed with an offer of financing. A potential applicant should always be able to demonstrate in the proposal that the company has handled this type of transaction before and has the skills available to control and complete the transaction. The fact that the transaction is of a size that is substantially larger than the previous ones is far less important, if it can be shown that the type of transaction has been undertaken regularly by the company in its normal course of business.

Why an institution should become involved

In considering such types of applications the institution is backing the management to a very high degree and relying upon its skills to react and produce answers to problems that may not have yet materialised. It is very similar to a development capital transaction and the qualities of the management are critical.

If we now return to the property development transaction: if it had not been possible for the company to find further security then the bank may still have expressed a wish to proceed in certain circumstances. You will recall that the bank would lend up to 70% of the cost of the development on a conventional basis, but if the bank was convinced about the attributes of the scheme, then it may suggest that it could make available 100% on a joint venture basis, possibly taking some limited guarantees from the company.

For such a venture the bank may seek 50% of the profit of the transaction as well as a return on its loan. This of course is a significant shift in the bank's position and for this transaction it is entering into a business partnership with its client. This is an example of what are sometimes referred to as merchant banking transactions. Traditionally merchant banks had small balance sheets and utilised them sparingly on high-reward transactions (I hasten to add that this was before the days of investment banks spanning the cosmos and trading round the clock).

Reducing the risk

Another example of these types of transaction is providing funds for a team to purchase a work of art and then selling it at a higher price. The institution is relying upon the skills of the team to pay the right price and also have the right contacts to dispose of the property at a profit. A variation might also be providing a loan to a company for bridging a rights issue, in other words the company intends to raise finance by making an issue of shares, but this can be an uncertain process as it relies upon the external situation and in particular the state of the market at the time. It is sometimes possible to obtain interim funding from an institution until the issue can be made and the loan repaid. This is often only possible if the lending institution is also undertaking the rights issue through its corporate finance department, so that it can exercise adequate control and fully understand the likelihood of the rights issue being made. This type of loan would not normally warrant a profit share arrangement but it would command a higher interest rate because of its unusual nature and the scarcity of institutions willing to provide it.

I can remember several years ago putting together a syndicate to bid for a certain horse if it won a particular race, the idea being that it would then be put out to stud and the fees received used to pay the interest and capital on the loan. In fact it did not win, therefore the facility was never required; but although the research and verification that went into the project were considerable, in the end it was necessary to rely upon the opinion of a group of breeders and also their skills, to persuade that the project was viable and could generate the necessary cash to produce a satisfactory reward. However, what this example serves to illustrate is the unusual nature of the security which was offered, namely a charge over the horse itself. This was not immediately regarded as good security and can easily be seen to be fraught with potential problems; nevertheless by serious analysis of the risks it was then possible to assess which of them were unacceptable and which were unpleasant but could be lived with. When the unacceptable risks had been listed, we then set about trying to eliminate them and we were surprised to find that what we originally regarded as major concerns could be insured in the Lloyds market for quite a small premium. This recourse to other markets to remove risks is not an unusual one and can be seen in any standard mortgage facility, which always requires the borrower to maintain insurance to remove the risks of fire and storm damage etc. Similarly it is often possible to arrange insurance for the middle slice of risk in a property development transaction by the payment of relatively small premiums. For example, suppose the bank only wished to lend 70% of the development costs of a project but in reality what was really required was 85% of the development costs because the potential borrower only had 15% to put down. It may be possible for the bank to lend 85% but seek to reinsure the risk of the difference between the 70% loan which the bank wished to make and the 85% which is required. To do this the bank would approach an insurance company with details about the project, and also details about the bank's client, which would be considered by the insurance company; in particular, the insurance company would concentrate upon the ability of the development company to perform, rather than its financial standing. If the insurance company felt satisfied with the project and comfortable with the development company, then it would offer to take the risk of the 15% loan from the bank for the payment of a flat fee, say, 0.5%. Unfortunately the property market moves in cycles and the availability of these guarantees rather depends upon the stage of the cycle, ie they are available in rising markets but difficult to obtain in falling ones.

Similarly projects such as the financing of films can rely heavily upon the insurance of certain risks. When an institution makes a loan available to finance a project such as a film it is in the rather unenviable position of not having a tangible asset to take as security until the film is finally complete and in the can. It does not take a great deal of imagination to identify the sorts of risk that might arise and prevent a film from being completed. As a result of this there are certain companies that provide what are called completion guarantees. This means that for the payment of an insurance premium they will undertake to provide a guarantee that the film will be finished even if they have to take over the production themselves. Fortunately these guarantees are very rarely called upon but they are considered to be a very useful product.

Other instances of insurance are residual value guarantees. These are normally provided on large items of plant or equipment which are being leased or for which, perhaps, a loan has to be made to purchase them. A similar type of facility is often encountered in the leasing of smaller vehicles or plant and this is often provided by the manufacturer or supplier and called a buy-back guarantee. In this case the manufacturer or supplier offers to buy back the vehicle at fixed values over given periods. For example, suppose a Leyland van is purchased for £7,000; for a small payment, say 2% of capital value, the manufacturer will undertake to buy the van back as follows:

After 12 months	£5,600
After 24 months	£4,200
After 36 months	£2,800

The manufacturer would probably specify that the vehicles would have had to only have an average mileage of, say, 16,000 miles pa and that they should be free from major defects ie cracked gearboxes etc. This sort of undertaking can go a long way to reducing the risk for the institution which is leasing the vehicles.

Suppose the leasing rental is paid quarterly and, as is normal, it is in advance; then if the rate charged is £75 per £1000 leased per quarter for four years then the quarterly rental is:

$$\text{£}7{,}000 \times \frac{75}{1000} = \text{£}525$$

Upon the customer signing the lease the bank pays £7,000 to acquire the vehicle and the customer pays the bank the first quarterly rental in advance, namely £525. When assessing its risk the bank knows that the manufacturers will repurchase the vehicle in 12 months' time for £5,600 because the bank has payed 2% of £7,000, ie £140, for a buy-back guarantee. In this case the maximum risk to the bank at the outset is:

$$\text{£}7{,}000 - \text{£}525 - \text{£}5{,}600 + \text{£}140 = \text{£}1{,}015$$

As can be seen, the maximum risk to the bank occurs at the beginning because after three months have elapsed the bank receives another payment of £525, therefore the risk then reduces to:

$$£1,015 - £525 = £490$$

The above calculations are not strictly accurate and have been simplified in that the costs of funds to the bank have been ignored to illustrate a point. In the second example the bank has had to bear the interest costs of its notional loan to the customer for three months, ie if a rate of 10% per annum is assumed then:

$$(£7,000 + £140 - £525) \times \frac{10}{100} \times \frac{3}{12} = £165$$

Then the exposure to the bank after three months is:

$$£1,015 - £525 + £165 = £655$$

Nevertheless it is clear that the provision of a buy-back guarantee allows the bank to reduce the level of exposure for a client from what would be £7,000 to considerably less. It should not be forgotten that there is now an additional risk created, because the buy-back guarantee is only as good as the covenant of the company giving it and the status of the manufacturer or dealer will need to be considered as well. This moving of risks for a fee may seem to be an easy way for an insurance company to earn money but it should be remembered that there have been instances of these types of policies being called upon and being found to be very expensive for the writers of the policies. A case in point is that of the so-called 'J' policies when insurance guarantees were being given for residual values on certain types of computer equipment. Unfortunately the computer market was moving very quickly and obsolescence in hardware began to occur within shorter and shorter time-frames. A result of this was that these policies, which were written at Lloyds, were required to enable lessors to provide a competitive lease, because with residual value guarantees they could in effect write operating leases knowing that they could get a guaranteed value for the hardware if they had to repossess it and sell it because the lessee had defaulted. Unfortunately lessees did default and the guarantees were called upon and the insurance underwriters could not get a high enough price for the equipment to recover the full guarantee costs.

A much-used form of insurance is that provided by the Export Credit Guarantee Department, a government body that will provide insurance against specific risks for exporters of goods from the United Kingdom. It is possible to obtain insurance against a purchaser defaulting or against unfair calling of contract bonds; these enable some of the unknowns to be taken out of transactions. There are also private insurance companies which operate in the United Kingdom and will provide insurance against the insolvency of debtors in the United Kingdom and variations upon this theme which also can prove extremely useful in structuring deals into a form where they can be acceptable to one institution or another.

This may seem to be another detailed description of the sorts of risk for which it may be possible to obtain accommodation in other markets but it is sometimes only by using these techniques that it is possible to get the more unconventional type of financing requirements funded and it is only by fully analysing the risks that the project can be broken down into acceptable and unacceptable areas.

Where can they be funded?

At the beginning of this chapter I sought to identify the specific attributes that distinguished this class of unconventional short-term funding requirements and, while I believe that this is possible, it is extremely difficult to go on further and define them in any other manner than by giving specific examples that will serve to illustrate the type of eventualities that may give rise to these transactions.

Having done this the next question that may reasonably be asked is what kind of institution will be available to provide financing. Here I would stress that there is no guaranteed financier, as it depends very much upon the strategies that an institution is following at the time and these transactions are, at best, more often regarded as marginal, perhaps only to be undertaken a few times in exceptional circumstances and for well-known customers. This is understandable because the risks are much higher than conventional financing and standard development capital institutions are just not geared up to taking these sorts of risk, even though they may seem more suited to the types of risk taken in that sector. This may at first seem a strange reaction and it may seem that development capitalists are passing up a good opportunity to make money; however upon closer examination it may be seen that this is not necessarily the case. A development capital institution is normally established to invest in unquoted companies with a view to achieving either a running yield or a capital gain. When confronted with this statement most development capital companies would reply that it was far too narrow a definition and that they were in business to make money for their shareholders. This may be so, but they are only equipped to take risks by buying shares in unquoted companies and it is because the institutional approach to development capital is precisely this approach that in this area they are extremely inflexible. They do not have the resources to consider how best a client with a letter of credit for a large contract may be financed to undertake it and what the level of reward should be. The way a development capital company would solve this is by some device which involved the equity of the client and this would be a very expensive transaction for the client and still be in place when the contract had been completed. To understand the type of transaction referred to above, what is needed is a practical knowledge of banking, as found in a commercial banker, and an analytical ability similar to that used when evaluating an equity investment; but what is then required is the ability to structure a short-term facility with an appropriate reward, ie linked to the profit to be made. This combination of skills and the desire to take these risks are probably only present within the merchant banking sector and, as I have mentioned before, I draw a distinction between merchant and investment banking. What is required is a banker who knows his client, understands the risks and has the ability to ensure that his institution can underwrite them. It may be possible to find this in the occasional branch of a clearing bank where the manager is operating within his own sanctioning authority, but it is a very rare occurrence. The best chances of success are somewhere among the medium-sized merchant banks in the City of London. I would suggest that an approach is made at no lower than assistant director level.

Chapter 8

CONSTRUCTING THE FINANCING PROPOSAL

We can now consider what is involved in constructing the financing proposal. This is a very important part of the presentation to the bank but as can be seen from previous discussions it is only part of what needs to be done and understood if an effective proposal is to be constructed and presented. It will incorporate a business plan but this in itself is not necessarily a request for finance. In the circumstances we are discussing we assume that the business plan shows a funding need, otherwise there would be no need to make a presentation to a bank, but a business plan is merely a set of assumptions about a business projected forward over a period of time within the framework of a financial model expressing certain aspects of the business, eg the relationship between sales and overheads. The business plan then shows what amounts of cash are required by the business if those assumptions are made. What a financing proposal has to do as well to be most effective is take the cash shortfall, if there is one, then decide what would be the desirable structure from the company's viewpoint for funding taking all aspects of the business into account including uncertainty. For example, there is no point suggesting a structure for all of the finance to be on overdraft if it is clearly not attractive to a bank to provide this sort of facility. It is far more sensible to decide the mix of debt and equity and then present this to the bank or institution which is most suitable for your requirements. There may be several in certain circumstances.

Before constructing any series of arguments it is normally more efficient if some time is spent thinking and planning what will be contained in them and how they will inter-relate with each other in strengthening the argument. The presentation will be most effective if it is clearly directed at a specific target, ie understand what it is that you are asking for, how much, for how long and in what form. If you can clearly demonstrate this then you should be well placed to argue why it is worthwhile for a bank to provide it. It is therefore worthwhile sketching out the plan in note form before you start and identifying the key arguments and information requirements that will go into each section. This is not only a good discipline for constructing the document but it also serves as a checklist to ensure that all relevant matters are included. It can also be used to determine what information will be required and where it will have to come from. This in turn will give you an idea of the resources that you will need to deploy in completing the proposal and the likely timescale that will be required. The length of the proposal is something that is determined by how complex the proposition is and how dependent it is upon the success of the project to be financed. Clearly, if your business is seeking a loan for a fairly complex process that involves several highly technical areas and the business can support the loan comfortably on the basis of its existing earnings then it would not be necessary to provide much detail other than a broad overview of the new project because the bank would not need to understand a detailed review of this and its viability before being able to decide whether they wish to provide funding. However, should the success of the project be critical in enabling the company to repay the facility then by definition it will be some form of equity risk and the bank would need to understand the arguments fully before feeling confident about advancing any funds. As a rule of thumb, presentations vary between 20 and 50 pages although they can have quite substantial appendices depending upon the circumstances of the company.

The elements of the proposal — checklist

The following headings will serve as a checklist of the major areas to be included in a proposal. Naturally each business will have particular areas peculiar to itself and these will need to be expanded where relevant. However, if any of the areas mentioned below are not included in your proposal you should have a good reason why it is necessary to leave them out. Where appropriate I have indicated on the left hand side of the page the sorts of areas that should be covered under the headings on the right-hand side of the pages.

Contents of the appraisal

(1) Overview/executive summary - Requirement
- History

	- Markets
	- Products
	- Company philosophy/corporate strategy
	- Projections
	- Advantages/peculiar skills
(2) Introduction	- What the company is doing
	- How it arrived at this point
	- Why it wishes to undertake the new project
	- What it sees as the longer-term objectives
	- Details of the financial structure being requested
(3) Product description	- Individual products
	- Production processes detailed
	- Production scheduling
(4) Market analysis	- General overview
	- Sector analysis
	- Product analysis
	- Competition
	- Product life cycles
(5) Marketing strategy	- Distribution
	- Pricing policy
	- Advertising and promotion
(6) Sales forecasts	- Built up by product/sector
(7) Description of new project	
(8) Staffing requirements	
(9) Management structure	
(10) Systems	- Management information systems operating within the company

(11) Financial information summarised	- Last three years' audited accounts - Projections, balance sheet and cash flow - Sensitivities
(12) Appendices	- Relevant documents in full - Last three years' management accounts - Three years' projections, balance sheet, profit and loss and cash flow - Sensitivity analyses - Detailed financing structure - Assumptions for projections - Key management curriculum vitae - Product brochures - Press comment etc.

1 The overview/executive summary

From our early discussions it should be clear that the overview or summary is an important sales aid for the proposition. It should enable the banker to obtain a broad view of the proposal very quickly in order that he can then decide whether to take the matter further and read the full plan. It should therefore be capable of inducing a certain amount of interest as well as just being a collection of facts. To do this it needs to reflect the personalities of the people involved. What it should not do is contain arguments and seek to substantiate facts — this is the purpose of the full plan. The banker will assume that if a statement is made in the overview, then it can be supported and will be dealt with in the body of the document.

If the summary is poor your chances of success will be jeopardised because it can easily be assumed that that is the quality of the underlying proposal and the busier someone is the more likely they are to use this method of rejection. Remember that your proposal and business plan is not the business you are running: it is a description of that business and its aspirations. The business could be extremely sound and energetic but if that is not conveyed in the proposal at a very early stage, ie in the summary, the reader who does not know your operation could lose interest and your opportunity might be lost. If you have a reasonably large business plan the summary can be an extremely useful document to present to institutions first of all to talk about the business and the proposal. It is very difficult to have a coherent conversation when jumping around in a weighty business plan because it is not always possible to keep sight of the overall arguments and objectives. It could be that initially an institution will only ask to see a copy of the summary and base its decision about proceeding to the next stage purely on the views it forms from that document. Therefore I cannot emphasise enough the importance of this aspect of the proposition. The summary length will vary depending upon the size of the business plan. It could vary from one or two pages to seven or eight. Hopefully, it will not be much longer because then it ceases to fulfil its primary purpose, which is to be a summary, and it then becomes a less detailed plan which still requires a considerable amount of time to get to grips with.

The summary should contain a brief description of the purpose of the proposition, that is, the amount of funding that is being requested, when it is required by, how long it will be required for and in what form the company is seeking to raise it, ie debt or equity. It is generally not a good idea to suggest interest rates or percentage of equity at this stage because the primary purpose is to create an interest in the business. Then after this is established details like that can be negotiated. It should also indicate why the financing requirement has arisen and the purpose to which the funds will be put. The institution then knows very quickly what it is being asked to look at and what the funds will be used for. Details about returns etc. come later on.

After establishing the reasons for the proposal it is appropriate to outline the history of the business giving any salient points about its development over the years. Clearly, unless these are exceptional events which happened more than five years ago it is unlikely to be of significant importance to this proposition and should not be included in the summary. It is helpful if a brief summary of the trading of the business can be given over the last three to five years and how this is presented will depend upon the nature of the business. If there are several clearly defined areas of activity it may well be helpful to show how the sales and profits generated from these areas combined to make up the total turnover and profit for each year shown. What these should not be is a detailed breakdown of costs and revenues as these are not appropriate in the summary. As a general rule only sales, interest charges, pre-tax profits, tax charge, profit after tax and distributions should be indicated.

Having dealt with what the company has been doing for the last few years it is then logical to explain the marketplace where it is now operating and the products that it is offering in those markets. It is difficult to establish a rule for whether products should be discussed before markets or vice versa and it should always be taken as what seems logical for each individual case. However, it is important that the institution is given a broad description of the company's perception of the market in which it operates, size, where it exists and how it will grow or contract. Then, within this marketplace, what are the particular products that the company produces, what market share it has of each of the individual markets and what particular processes it uses to create its products. Clearly this has to be tailored when discussing service industries but the principles are the same. It can often be helpful if one or two close competitors are defined as this can then help to establish the company's position. However, if they are obscure companies that would not generally be known, it is probably not worth mentioning them in the summary.

The company's philosophy in the marketplaces and the particular skills it considers itself to possess are important factors from the institution's viewpoint as it gives an insight into what the company sees as setting itself apart from its competition and what it sees as its major objectives in the future. It should also be clear from this section how the financing requirements fit in with and assist the company in achieving these long-term objectives.

Then a summary of the projections for profit and loss and cash flows over the next two or three years can be given indicating the amount of existing facilities and the anticipated requirements on a quarterly basis. It is helpful if projections can include outline balance sheets as these help to support the previous figures and show the shape of the company if it follows a proposed course of action. The aim of this section is to give the institution an idea of what sorts of rewards are likely to be obtained if the new funds are introduced into the business, and whether it is likely to find this an attractive level of remuneration obviously depends upon the way in which the funds are to be provided.

As a final inclusion to the summary it can be useful to provide a section on key management explaining their roles and responsibilities with an indication of the management structure. Brief details on background are sometimes appropriate in a longer summary, otherwise simply refer to the details given in the appendices.

When a banker has read the summary he should be in no doubt about what he is being asked to do, what the business has been doing, where it wants to go and what the particular rewards may be. If when someone reads the summary there is doubt over any one of these areas it must be rectified.

2 Introduction

This is the beginning of the business plan. Everything that follows should be entirely self-contained and not rely upon references and information given in the summary. It should be capable of being read and there should be no loss of understanding if the summary were to be destroyed. The purpose of this section is to set the scene for the institution so that there is a knowledge level before more basic considerations of the arguments. Simplicity and clarity of thought are paramount when constructing a business plan. Otherwise there is a loss of impact for the points which you wish to emphasise. This theme must run throughout the document and it can be useful to number each section and have sub-references for each paragraph. This assists in locating sections and classifies points into distinct groupings. There is no absolutely right way of constructing a plan and determining how much should be included or left out. What matters is that after someone has read your plan they should be sure what you are seeking and why.

As a general guide, I would expect to read in an introduction a brief description of the history of the company with any points expanded which are important to the proposal. For example, if there was a merger between two companies ten years ago which produced two shareholder blocks which are now at odds with each other this would now be a significant point which needed to be understood. If, however, all that happened as a result of the merger was an increase in the turnover of the business but exactly the same products were being produced, then only a passing reference needs to be made. The purpose of the brief history of the business is to explain how the business and the management come to the point they are now at.

This history can then be developed into the present day with a description of the business as it currently is in terms of resources, ie factory sites, employees, key management and products. These need to be explained in terms of industry, product areas and marketplaces. This will then bring the institution completely up to date and the rationale for the project — be it money for increasing working capital or constructing a new factory — can then be explained in the context of where the company finds itself, what its strengths and weaknesses are and what its longer-term objectives may be. It then needs to be explained how, by undertaking this particular project, it will be assisting in achieving these longer-term objectives and perhaps what the consequences of the particular course of action might be, eg if a new factory is being built it may well be the first step in several new factories given that this one is successful.

Having described the new project it is helpful and instructive to have an indication from the company how it wishes to fund the project and the form that this funding might take. There is no need for this to be a very sophisticated plan but a broad indication is helpful. A simple table setting out the structure will suffice, eg:

Total requirement	£500,000
Equity	£200,000
Term loan	£200,000
(period five years equal annual repayments)	
Overdraft	£100,000

This will enable the institution to see how you are approaching the problem.

3 Product description
This section should provide the institution with a full appreciation of the company's product range. It is not necessary for this to be highly technical and consist of detailed engineering diagrams but sufficient information needs to be provided to enable the bank or institution to be able to identify the product. It can be helpful to include in the appendices such items as advertising leaflets and product brochures that the company produces and reference can then be made to them to help describe the product range.

The product description leads on to the processes employed to produce this product range, its physical location and the components required. Here the institution needs to understand whether it involves special techniques or components that are peculiar to your operation or whether it is a general process with many sources of supply for the various parts required. Items which may need to be touched upon are: the volatility of the processes to suppliers and components; whether it is possible to multi-source and whether there are exchange rate risks inherent in the process; what labour relations have been like; whether there are any particular skills which are difficult to obtain. The purpose should be to give a balanced view of the risks involved in undertaking these processes and the degree of flexibility that exists should there be short-term restrictions upon resources whether they are labour, supplies or premises.

A further factor which it is appropriate to consider under this section is that of production scheduling and how the loading of the line relates to the sales projections/orders. This is quite an important feature that it is worthwhile explaining in more detail.

4 Market analysis

The company's marketplace is an area that may be extremely well researched with substantial amounts of information available publicly, eg if it were the car industry or the oil industry. On the other hand it could be an area where there is no trade association or published data and the information can only be achieved by estimates and taking views on competitive positions. The availability of information has to be explained and the situation built up from the best information available. It is important that a feel for size of market is given as this allows the institution to place the company within the marketplace and obtain an indication for the potential that could exist. The general overview should deal with the broad trends of the marketplace and will address its growth or decline, eg whether it is a luxury or a basic commodity, and therefore whether increases in disposable income increase demand, or if it is dependent upon the existence of other products and if so what the determinants of demand for these products are.

Having defined the marketplace it is then probably necessary to subdivide the market into sections and explain these sections within which the company operates. For example, it could be that a company operated within the furniture business but its goods might be of high quality; handmade products that do not compete with the mass-produced lines and have an entirely different customer base. Consequently, the precise determinants of demand for the company's particular products need to be explained fully.

The relationship between product and sector can then be developed and the particular attributes that make the product appropriate to a particular sector and the competition that exists within each sector by-product need to be defined. Competitors should be clearly explained and their strengths and weaknesses examined and compared with the company's products in an objective manner. A further consideration which may vary in importance depending on the nature of the product is the product life cycle. This can best be illustrated by examples of previous products and what determines the demand, eg whether it is fashion, technology or longevity. This gives an impression as to how dynamic the marketplace is and whether there is a need to be continually re-packaging and re-presenting. An important part of the market analysis is the existing customer base and what impact this might have for future developments. For example, is there a heavy dependence on any particular customer, the loss of which would make the business vulnerable? Have they been good payers? Does the business tend to be repeat business or is it a single sale? It can be useful to show the spread of customers highlighting any that account for more than 5 per cent of the company's sales/profits.

5 Marketing strategy

This can be a difficult area to define as it will vary considerably from company to company. What it should cover is the areas that allow the products to be presented in the marketplace, what decisions are taken, how they are taken, how often they are reviewed and revised. For example, it can be critical as to how a product is distributed and why it is necessary to adopt certain techniques in certain countries. What could be successful in the UK may result in ruin in the US or Europe, eg it could be possible to deal directly with retail outlets in the UK if a business was operating there. However, for a large overseas market it may be only possible to tackle this successfully by dealing with a local distributor who then has his own retail outlets. How the company sets its prices and how often it has to review them, what the critical determinants are and how it decides before it sets them that they are profitable are all areas that need to be explained. Similarly, the approach taken to advertise and promote the company's product range should also be covered and justified. Again, this is a difficult area to tackle and a logical way of approaching it can be to structure it by product/sector.

6 Sales forecasts

Traditionally, this is the line which should drive the rest of the projections and the questions that will be asked by any institution are: is the projected income overstated, is it sustainable and why should sales grow if they are projected to do so? These are valid questions and need to be answered convincingly at this point. This can only be achieved by building up the forecasts and explaining the reasons for their projected levels. These reasons are a combination of factors which can be a function of various elements such as the following — the product, its quality, its pricing, research and development, its product life cycle, the competition and structure of the industry, why this product is special, what its particular strengths are, eg the product niche, do protections exist such as patents, the level of existing customers, whether these are likely to represent repeat orders, the level of the current order book and to what extent it underpins the level of sales being forecast. Other factors are whether there are any weaknesses such as sales forecasts being heavily dependent upon particular customers and if these are lost whether the level of sales can be substantiated or would be severely reduced, whether the business is seasonal, whether it is cyclical and if so what assumptions are being made about the state of the economy or the weather. It is not very convincing for a small business to say that because it expects the marketplace as a whole to grow by 5 per cent next year its sales should grow by a similar amount. The sales should be identified if possible by customer or group of customers and the sales force should be shown to be targeting these people. Sales forecasts have to be built up from the bottom, which is identifying individual customer requirements and arriving at a reasonable total which can then be viewed against expectations for the marketplace overall to see if there is an inconsistency.

7 Description of the new project

The rationale of the project needs to be restated and the timing it is seeking to achieve. This section may have to be a detailed review covering several areas in depth if it is a large operation and will need to include aspects such as sales forecasts, marketing, production, resources, suppliers, premises, funding and management. All these items should be covered in any proposition but obviously in some circumstances certain of these headings will not be developed except to mention that they have been considered and what the results are, eg if there is no new management requirement then this only needs stating whereas if a new factory were planned this would need explaining in some depth. If there is a separately identifiable business area, which may not always be the case, it can be useful to present this as an overlay on to the company's plans if the new project were not included. This can give a very easy appreciation of what the changes might entail were the new project to be undertaken. It is useful also to give an indication of the critical steps in the project. If new equipment is required it could be that there is a six month lead time for ordering the equipment. Therefore this order has to be placed before the project is started and even if the project were not completed there would be a commitment to pay for this equipment.

8 Staffing requirements

This may be a critical area or not depending on the nature of the proposition. It can be useful to show the current staffing of the business if necessary by product area or function. It can be developed to show where any new staff are going to be required and the anticipated timing. Any training needs for recruitment particulars should be explained at this stage. It may be that certain staff have to be moved, in which case contingency plans for what would happen if they refused to go need to be explained.

9 Management structure

An organisation chart showing reporting lines of middle and senior management with particular responsibilities can explain very easily what the relationships are which exist between various functions. However, this will only be useful if this is a true representation of what happens and not a theoretical exercise for what might be considered desirable. This is a good opportunity to explain the roles of the key management team and any of the important middle management. The curriculum vitae should be in the appendices and can be referred to but the purpose is to show that the team is qualified, ambitious, experienced and can work together. It should also be possible to demonstrate that the team is complete and has goals which coincide with any potential investors/ lenders. Management is the most important ingredient to the ability of the firm to survive in the long term. All institutions are aware of this and this particular section should explain why a management team can run the business and achieve the forecasts shown in the business plan.

10 Systems

The information systems which are operating within the company should be described and in particular those which generate monthly management information describing the reports produced and their scope together with the forecasting system used. This can be placed in context by explaining what the management team do to estimate their cash and production requirements over the next three months and how accurate these estimates have proved to be. Other systems such as credit control can also be referred to here if appropriate.

11 Financial information summarised

Results for the last three years should be summarised; in other words the accounts should not be reproduced together with notes but instead a reasonably detailed profit and loss account and balance sheet should be presented after being adjusted for any items which are not relevant to the current business. These should then be projected forward for the next three years and they should be shown on a quarterly basis. A cash flow should also be presented on the same basis with reference made to the peaks in a quarter rather than the three month end position. Against this cash flow the anticipated banking facilities should be shown. It is important that these projections can easily be reconciled with the sales projections referred to earlier in the chapter.

12 Appendices

This section should contain any detailed documents which would detract from the main body of the plan. In particular there should be included the full last three years' audited accounts, hopefully without any auditor's qualifications. If there is a qualification this should be addressed in the body of the text. There should also be detailed financial projections, ie balance sheet, profit and loss and cash flows for the next three years with the first year being constructed on a monthly basis and the remaining two years on a quarterly basis.

The projections should also include a series of calculations which have been produced when the key variables have been changed. The critical variables are going to be different for each individual project but in every situation there are going to be factors that are critical to the operation being able to be carried through. This might be interest rates, timing of completion of a factory, obtaining orders, whatever; what needs to be shown is the degree of vulnerability that the business might have to these external factors and the possibility of still continuing and being profitable even though events do not go according to plan.

The other aspect which sensitivities show up is the amount of additional facilities that might be required should there be a hiccup in the company's plans. This is important for an institution as it is probable that when circumstances arise which require this extra funding the institution is going to be the only source where these funds are going to come from. A list should be given of the key assumptions used in constructing the projections. These may include items such as anticipated inflation rates, interest rates, rates of taxation, wage increases, terms of payment and collection of monies, bad debts, distribution policy, selling prices, costs of raw materials and fuel etc. The idea is that the institution can understand the assumptions made in constructing the projections and judge whether it considers these realistic and if not ask for a re-run using alternative values which it suggests. This is where sensitivities can be helpful because, for example, if it can be shown that a 30 per cent variance in interest rates is not going to affect the project significantly then it is going to matter less whether the views of the company and the institution agree precisely because this particular variable is not going to be critical in assessing the project.

Curriculum vitae for the key management team can be included in the appendices if they have not been shown elsewhere. These should not be unduly laborious but seek to give a balanced view of each individual indicating name, address, family status, education, employment history with more detail being given in current events rather than earlier ones. It should also include some indication of general interest. The aim of the curriculum vitae should be directed at showing why each member of the management team is qualified and experienced to do the job that they are doing.

Finally, it can be very useful to include copies of product brochures and any recent press comment on the company or the industry in which it operates if it is felt to be helpful in setting the background to the business.

Examples of the layout for the projected balance sheets, profit and loss accounts and cash flows are shown below. Figures have been inserted in some of the columns by way of example:

(a) Summary of projected balance sheets

(b) Projected quarterly balance sheets

(c) Summary of projected profit and loss accounts

(d) Projected monthly profit and loss accounts for year one

(e) Projected quarterly profit and loss accounts for years two and three

(f) Projected monthly cash flow year one

(g) Projected quarterly cash flow years two and three

Summary of projected balance sheets

	Year 1 £'000's	*Year 2* £'000's	*Year 3* £'000's
FIXED ASSETS			
Cost	200	-	-
Less accumulated depreciation	40	-	-
	160	-	-
CURRENT ASSETS			
Stocks and work in progress	60	-	-
Debtors	40	-	-
Bank and cash	20	-	-
	120	-	-
CURRENT LIABILITIES			
Trade creditors	70	-	-
Tax	-	-	-
Bank overdraft	10	-	-
Current part of medium-term loan	10	-	-
	90	-	-
NET CURRENT ASSETS	30	-	-
TOTAL ASSETS LESS THAN CURRENT LIABILITIES	190	-	-
MEDIUM-TERM LOAN	50	-	-
NET ASSETS	140	-	-
CAPITAL RESERVES			
Share capital	90	-	-
Accumulated profits	50	-	-
	140	-	-
STATISTICS			
Net worth (shareholders' funds)	140	-	-
Debt to equity percentage (gearing)	50%	-	-
Current ratio (current assets/current liabilities)	1.3	-	-

Projected quarterly balance sheets

	Year 1				*Year 2*			
Quarter	1	2	3	4	1	2	3	4
FIXED ASSETS								
Cost	150	160	180	200	-	-	-	-
Less accumulated depreciation	10	15	25	40	-	-	-	-
	140	145	155	160	-	-	-	-
CURRENT ASSETS								
Stocks and work in progress	30	50	40	60	-	-	-	-
Debtors	20	30	35	40	-	-	-	-
Bank and cash	40	25	25	20	-	-	-	-
	90	105	100	120	-	-	-	-
CURRENT LIABILITIES								
Trade creditors	40	60	50	70	-	-	-	-
Tax	-	-	-	-	-	-	-	-
Bank overdraft	0	0	0	10	-	-	-	-
Current part of medium-term loan	10	10	10	10	-	-	-	-
	50	70	60	90	-	-	-	-
NET CURRENT ASSETS	40	35	40	30	-	-	-	-
TOTAL ASSETS LESS CURRENT LIABILITIES	180	180	195	190	-	-	-	-
MEDIUM-TERM LOAN	60	60	60	50	-	-	-	-
NET ASSETS	120	120	135	140	-	-	-	-

CAPITAL AND RESERVE								
Share capital	90	90	90	90	-	-	-	-
Accumulated profits	30	30	45	50	-	-	-	-
	120	120	135	140	-	-	-	-
STATISTICS								
Net worth (shareholders' funds)	120	120	135	140	-	-	-	-
Debt to equity percentage (gearing)	58%	58%	52%	50%	-	-	-	-
Current ratio (current assets/current liabilities)	2.2	1.5	1.7	1.3	-	-	-	-

Summary of projected profit and loss accounts

	Year 1 £'000's	*Year 2* £'000's	*Year 3* £'000's
SALES	1,500	-	-
COST OF SALES			
Materials	500	-	-
Labour	250	-	-
Other production costs	150	-	-
	900	-	-
GROSS PROFIT	600	-	-
OPERATING EXPENSES			
Marketing	250	-	-
Research and development	150	-	-
General and administrative	140	-	-
Depreciation	30	-	-
	570	-	-
PROFIT BEFORE INTEREST	30	-	-
Interest income (charge)	10	-	-
PROFIT BEFORE TAXATION	20	-	-
Taxation	-	-	-
NET PROFIT	20	-	-
EXPRESSED AS PERCENTAGES	%	%	%
SALES	100.0	-	-
COST OF SALES			
Materials	33.3	-	-
Labour	16.7	-	-
Other production costs	10.0	-	-
GROSS PROFIT	60.0	-	-
OPERATING EXPENSES	40.0	-	-
Marketing	16.7	-	-
Research and development	10.0	-	-
General administrative	9.3	-	-
Depreciation	2.0	-	-
	38.0	-	-
PROFIT BEFORE INTEREST	2.0	-	-
Interest charge	0.7	-	-
NET PROFIT	1.3	-	-

Projected monthly profit and loss accounts

Year 1

£'000's

Month	1	2	3	4	5	6	7	8	9	10	11	12	Total
SALES	-	-	-	-	-	-	-	-	-	-	-	-	1,500
COST OF SALES													
Materials	-	-	-	-	-	-	-	-	-	-	-	-	500
Labour	-	-	-	-	-	-	-	-	-	-	-	-	250
Other production costs	-	-	-	-	-	-	-	-	-	-	-	-	150
													900
	-	-	-	-	-	-	-	-	-	-	-	-	900
GROSS PROFIT	-	-	-	-	-	-	-	-	-	-	-	-	600
OPERATING EXPENSES													
Marketing	-	-	-	-	-	-	-	-	-	-	-	-	250
Research and development	-	-	-	-	-	-	-	-	-	-	-	-	150
General and administrative		-	-	-	-	-	-	-	-	-	-	-	140
Depreciation	-	-	-	-	-	-	-	-	-	-	-	-	30
	-	-	-	-	-	-	-	-	-	-	-	-	570
PROFIT BEFORE INTEREST	-	-	-	-	-	-	-	-	-	-	-	-	30
Interest (charge) income	-	-	-	-	-	-	-	-	-	-	-	-	10
NET PROFIT	-	-	-	-	-	-	-	-	-	-	-	-	20

EXPRESSED AS PERCENTAGES	%	%	%	%	%	%	%	%	%	%	%	%	%
SALES	-	-	-	-	-	-	-	-	-	-	-	-	-
COST OF SALES													
Materials	-	-	-	-	-	-	-	-	-	-	-	-	33.3
Labour	-	-	-	-	-	-	-	-	-	-	-	-	16.7
Other production costs	-	-	-	-	-	-	-	-	-	-	-	-	10.0
	-	-	-	-	-	-	-	-	-	-	-	-	60.0
GROSS PROFIT	-	-	-	-	-	-	-	-	-	-	-	-	40.0
OPERATING EXPENSES													
Marketing	-	-	-	-	-	-	-	-	-	-	-	-	16.7
Research and development	-	-	-	-	-	-	-	-	-	-	-	-	10.0
General and administrative	-	-	-	-	-	-	-	-	-	-	-	-	9.3
Depreciation	-	-	-	-	-	-	-	-	-	-	-	-	2.0
	-	-	-	-	-	-	-	-	-	-	-	-	38.0
PROFIT BEFORE INTEREST	-	-	-	-	-	-	-	-	-	-	-	-	2.0
Interest (charge) income	-	-	-	-	-	-	-	-	-	-	-	-	0.7
NET PROFIT	-	-	-	-	-	-	-	-	-	-	-	-	1.3

Projected quarterly profit and loss accounts

	Year 2		£'000's			*Year 3*				
Quarter	1	2	3	4	*Total*	1	2	3	4	*Total*
SALES	-	-	-	-	-	-	-	-	-	-
COST OF SALES										
Materials	-	-	-	-	-	-	-	-	-	-
Labour	-	-	-	-	-	-	-	-	-	-
Other production costs	-	-	-	-	-	-	-	-	-	-
	-	-	-	-	-	-	-	-	-	-
GROSS PROFIT	-	-	-	-	-	-	-	-	-	-
OPERATING EXPENSES										
Marketing	-	-	-	-	-	-	-	-	-	-
Research and development	-	-	-	-	-	-	-	-	-	-
General and administrative	-	-	-	-	-	-	-	-	-	-
Depreciation	-	-	-	-	-	-	-	-	-	-
	-	-	-	-	-	-	-	-	-	-
PROFIT BEFORE INTEREST	-	-	-	-	-	-	-	-	-	-
Interest (charge) income	-	-	-	-	-	-	-	-	-	-
NET PROFIT	-	-	-	-	-	-	-	-	-	-

EXPRESSED AS PERCENTAGES	%	%	%	%	%	%	%	%	%	%
SALES	-	-	-	-	-	-	-	-	-	-
COST OF SALES										
Materials	-	-	-	-	-	-	-	-	-	-
Labour	-	-	-	-	-	-	-	-	-	-
Other production costs	-	-	-	-	-	-	-	-	-	-
	-	-	-	-	-	-	-	-	-	-
OPERATING EXPENSES										
Marketing	-	-	-	-	-	-	-	-	-	-
Research and development	-	-	-	-	-	-	-	-	-	-
General and administrative	-	-	-	-	-	-	-	-	-	-
Depreciation	-	-	-	-	-	-	-	-	-	-
	-	-	-	-	-	-	-	-	-	-
PROFIT BEFORE INTEREST	-	-	-	-	-	-	-	-	-	-
Interest (charge) income	-	-	-	-	-	-	-	-	-	-
NET PROFIT	-	-	-	-	-	-	-	-	-	-

Projected monthly cash flow

				Year 1									
						£'000's							
Month	1	2	3	4	5	6	7	8	9	10	11	12	*Total*
RECEIPTS													
Collection of sales	-	-	-	-	-	-	-	-	-	-	-	-	-
VAT on sales and receipts from Customs & Excise	-	-	-	-	-	-	-	-	-	-	-	-	-
	-	-	-	-	-	-	-	-	-	-	-	-	-
PAYMENTS													
Accounts payable	-	-	-	-	-	-	-	-	-	-	-	-	-
VAT on expenditure and payments to Customs & Excise	-	-	-	-	-	-	-	-	-	-	-	-	-
	-	-	-	-	-	-	-	-	-	-	-	-	-
OUTFLOW FROM TRADING	-	-	-	-	-	-	-	-	-	-	-	-	-
CAPITAL EXPENDITURE	-	-	-	-	-	-	-	-	-	-	-	-	-
Net interest (payment) income		-	-	-	-	-	-	-	-	-	-	-	-
NET CASH OUTFLOW	-	-	-	-	-	-	-	-	-	-	-	-	-
OPENING BALANCE	-	-	-	-	-	-	-	-	-	-	-	-	-
CLOSING BALANCE	-	-	-	-	-	-	-	-	-	-	-	-	-

Projected quarterly cash flow

	Year 2				£'000's	Year 3				
Quarter	1	2	3	4	Total	1	2	3	4	Total
RECEIPTS										
Collection of sales	-	-	-	-	-	-	-	-	-	-
VAT on sales and receipts from Customs & Excise	-	-	-	-	-	-	-	-	-	-
	-	-	-	-	-	-	-	-	-	-
PAYMENTS										
Accounts payable	-	-	-	-	-	-	-	-	-	-
VAT on expenditure and payments to Customs & Excise	-	-	-	-	-	-	-	-	-	-
	-	-	-	-	-	-	-	-	-	-
OUTFLOW FROM TRADING	-	-	-	-	-	-	-	-	-	-
CAPITAL EXPENDITURE	-	-	-	-	-	-	-	-	-	-
Net interest (payment) income	-	-	-	-	-	-	-	-	-	-
NET CASH OUTFLOW	-	-	-	-	-	-	-	-	-	-
OPENING BALANCE	-	-	-	-	-	-	-	-	-	-
CLOSING BALANCE										

Chapter 9

PRESENTING THE APPLICATION

Selection of the institution

Having now reached a stage where the application has been prepared and is in the form where it is considered to represent the objectives of the business and the aspirations of the management it needs to be presented to an appropriate institution. The institution should be selected bearing in mind the financing instruments which you envisage that you will require. If you are not certain which institutions are available then by contacting either your accountant or business adviser you should be able to obtain an idea of which ones are operating in your particular area. If it is equity investment that you require, a list of members can be obtained from the British Venture Capital Association which should provide you with a considerable selection to choose from. In addition, there are quite often lists of development capital companies in financial magazines such as *The Investors Chronicle* where there is also an indication of the type of investments undertaken. Your bank manager can also provide you with an introduction to a development capital house but bear in mind that all of the large banking operations have their own development capital operations and therefore they will probably be anxious to introduce you to that particular organisation. I would say that all of these institutions are very professional and competent. Another source of information is the local Chamber of Commerce and almost all professional advisers will be aware of most of the facilities available locally. However, if it can be achieved, personal recommendation of an institution is the best way of finding out first hand how it has dealt with its clients and, if you can locate someone who has dealt with the particular institution you are thinking of, using this can be a very useful source of information.

It is sensible not to approach too many institutions with your proposal but to select no more than two or three and stay with these initially. The financial world can be very small at times and if institutions hear from their associates about one particular proposal it can give the impression that it is being 'hawked around' as a result of it being of poor quality. This would prejudice any manager who has not yet seen it and jeopardise the chances of success if he is to be approached later.

Preparation

Identify two or three institutions and make approaches to them initially by telephone. In your telephone conversation you will be seeking to interest the manager in seeing your document. Therefore have a clear idea in your mind how you are going to convey the salient points of your proposal in a short conversation. You should provide him with an idea of:

- What you do
- How profitable you are
- How much you require
- What you require it for
- What the returns will be
- What type of funding you are seeking

If that interests him he will ask to see your proposal and you have started on the first stage of your mission. It can be useful to offer to send a summary first if your plan is a fairly bulky document.

To prevent any mistakes or misunderstandings keep a list of the institutions you approach together with the names and addresses of the people you speak to and the action you have agreed to take or that they have agreed to take. It can also be useful to number your documents so that you can keep track of them. If you have sent a document out and have heard nothing then you should follow it up after a reasonable time to ensure that it has been received.

Response

Do not expect an institution to react instantaneously. Remember that you have been working on the application for some time and are completely familiar with it. It can take a week from receiving the document for an institution to give an initial reaction and this may be only to ask you to come in for a meeting to talk about it.

This is a favourable sign and before you go to the meeting ensure that you are prepared and keep any points that you make short and pertinent to the question being asked. It is very easy for a manager to be put off because every time he asks a question he gets a ten minute reply. Under no circumstances turn up for a meeting with a proposal under your arm and expect to discuss it if the institution has not seen it before. This is giving yourself the worst possible chance of success. As we have mentioned earlier, people need to familiarise themselves with the proposal so that they feel comfortable with it. This is also true about the timing of asking for funding. Do not leave it until the last minute so that you are constantly pressing the institution because you are desperate for the funds. Institutions can move very quickly when required to but this costs money because people have to be taken off other activities and it does not create a set of circumstances where decisions can be made giving full weight to arguments. When in a hurry there is a tendency to tread cautiously because everyone knows that this is when mistakes are made and therefore there is a tendency to compensate for this by being more prudent than normal.

I would therefore summarise by saying, give the bank the best opportunity to help you and you can do this by:

- Understanding your bank's approach to risk reward
- Ensuring that your presentation is directed towards the risks and rewards in the proposition
- Arriving fully prepared for the questions that will be asked
- Allowing time for the bank's decision-making process

If these guidelines are adhered to then the objectives will be achieved to ensure that the proposition receives the full attention it deserves and is judged on its merits and that these merits are not detracted from by the quality of the presentation.

Remember, the bank wants to do business with you.

INDEX